MEMORIAL DRIVE

MEMORIAL DRIVE

A Daughter's Memoir

NATASHA TRETHEWEY

BLOOMSBURY CIRCUS
LONDON · OXFORD · NEW YORK · NEW DELHI · SYDNEY

BLOOMSBURY PUBLISHING
Bloomsbury Publishing Plc
50 Bedford Square, London, WC1B 3DP, UK

BLOOMSBURY, BLOOMSBURY PUBLISHING and the Diana logo
are trademarks of Bloomsbury Publishing Plc

First published in 2020 in the USA by Ecco, HarperCollins
First published in Great Britain 2020

A catalogue record for this book is available from the British Library

ISBN: HB: 978-1-4088-4001-6; TPB: 978-1-4088-4002-3;
eBook: 978-1-4088-4003-0

2 4 6 8 10 9 7 5 3

4 6 8 10 9 7 5 3

Text design by Renata de Oliveira
Printed and bound in Great Britain by CPI Group (UK) Ltd, Croydon CR0 4YY

To find out more about our authors and books visit
www.bloomsbury.com and sign up for our newsletters

In memory of the women who made me:
FRANCES DIXON INGRAHAM
LERETTA DIXON TURNBOUGH
and
GWENDOLYN ANN TURNBOUGH (NÉE),
my mother

The past beats inside me like a second heart.
                    —JOHN BANVILLE, *THE SEA*

All journeys have secret destinations of which the traveler is unaware.   —MARTIN BUBER

CONTENTS

II.

I.

[   ]

Three weeks after my mother is dead I dream of her: We walk
a rutted path, an oval track around which we are making our
slow revolution: side by side, so close our shoulders nearly touch,
neither of us speaking, both of us in our traces. Though I know
she is dead I have a sense of contentment, as if she's only gone
someplace else to which I've journeyed to meet her. The world
around us is dim, a backdrop of shadows out of which, now, a
man comes. Even in the dream I know what he has done, and yet
I smile, lifting my hand and speaking a greeting as he passes. It's
then that my mother turns to me, then that I see it: a hole, the
size of a quarter, in the center of her forehead. From it comes a
light so bright, so piercing, that I suffer the kind of momentary
blindness brought on by staring at the sun—her face nothing but
light ringed in darkness when she speaks: "Do you know what
it means to have a wound that never heals?" I know I am not
meant to answer and so we walk on as before, rounding the
path until we meet him again. This time he's come to finish what
he started: holding a gun, he is aiming at her head. This time I
think I can save her. Is it enough to throw myself in the bullet's
path? Shout "No!"? I wake to that single word, my own
voice wrenching me from sleep. But it's my mother's voice
that remains, her last question to me—"Do you know what it
means to have a wound that never heals?"—a refrain.

PROLOGUE

THE LAST IMAGE OF MY MOTHER, BUT FOR THE photographs taken of her body at the crime scene, is the formal portrait made only a few months before her death. She sat for it in a mass-market studio known for its competent but unremarkable pictures: babies coaxed to laughter by hand puppets, children in stair-step formation wearing matching Christmas sweaters—all against a common backdrop. Sometimes it's a sky-blue scrim that looks as if it's been brushed with a feather, or an autumn scene of red and yellow leaves framing a post-and-rail fence. For moodier portraits, as if to convey a sense of seriousness or formal elegance, there's the plain black scrim.

She was forty years old. For the sitting she'd chosen a long-sleeved black sheath, the high collar open at the throat. She does not look at the camera, her eyes fixed at a point in the distance that seems to be just above my head, making her face as inscrutable as it always was—her high, elegant forehead, smooth and unlined, a billboard upon which nothing is written. Nor does she smile, which makes the cleft in her chin more pronounced, her jawline softly squared above her slender neck. She sits perfectly erect without looking forced or uncomfortable. Perhaps she intended to look back on it years later and say, "That's where it began, my new life." I am struck with the thought that this is what she must have meant to do: document herself as a woman come this far, the rest of her life ahead of her.

The thought of that has always filled me with despair, and so for years I chose other stories to tell myself. In one version, she knew she would soon be killed. I know she had gone to see a psychic for entertainment with some friends from work; she'd told me as much, though she never said what she'd learned. Around that time she had also taken out several life insurance policies, and so for years I told myself she must have been preparing for the inevitable, making sure—in her last few weeks—that her children would be taken care of after she was gone.

In reality, if the psychic told her anything it was most likely something promising about her future—romance, perhaps, or hopeful predictions about the new job she'd just taken as personnel director for human resources at the county mental health agency. I know that most likely the life insurance policies were simply one of the benefits of that job: she'd have signed up for them during the open enrollment period for new employees. Still, the narrative of her making plans, stoically aware of what was to come, comforts me. I can't bear to think of the alternative, can't bear to think of her in that horrible moment, the sudden realization of her imminent death after allowing herself to believe she had escaped. Perhaps the truth lies somewhere between her hope and her pragmatism.

Hindsight makes me see the portrait differently now—how gloomy it is—as if the photographer meant to produce something artistic, rather than an ordinary studio portrait. It's as if he made of the negative space around her a frame to foreground some difficult knowledge: the dark past behind her, her face lit toward a future upon which her gaze is fixed.

And yet—undeniably—something else is there, elegiac even then: a strange corner of light just behind her head, perhaps the photographer's mistake, appearing as though a doorway has opened, a passage through which, turning, she might soon depart. Looking at it now, with all I know of what was to come, I see what else the photographer has done. He's shot her like this: her black dress black as the scrim behind her so that, but for her face, she is in fact part of that darkness, emerging from it as from the depths of memory.

_____

NEARLY THIRTY YEARS AFTER MY MOTHER'S DEATH I went back for the first time to the place she was murdered. I'd not been there since the year I turned nineteen, when I had to clean out her apartment, disposing of everything I could not—or would not—carry with me: all the furniture and household items, her clothing, her large collection of records. I kept only a few of her books, a heavy belt made of bullets, and a single plant she had loved—a dieffenbachia. Throughout my childhood it had been my responsibility to tend it, every week, dusting and misting the upper leaves and snipping the browned lower ones. *Be careful when you handle it,* my mother warned. A small precaution, seemingly unnecessary, but there is a toxin in the sap of the dieffenbachia; it oozes from the leaves and the stems where they are cut. *Dumb cane,* the plant is called, because it can cause a temporary inability to speak. *Struck dumb,* we say when fear or shock or astonishment renders us mute; *dumb grief,* when the grief is not expressed in uttered words. I could not then grasp the inherent metaphor of the plant, my relationship with my mother, what it would mean that she had made its care my duty, while warning me of its danger.

When I left Atlanta, vowing never to return, I took with me what I had cultivated all those years: mute avoidance of my past, silence and willed amnesia buried deep in me like a root. Nor could I have anticipated then that anything would ever draw me back to that city, to a geography that held at every turn a reminder of a past I was determined to forget even as I tried to honor her memory in every way I knew how. Indeed, going back for work, after accepting a university faculty position, I thought I could circumvent my former life, going out of my way to avoid at least the one place I could not bear to see. Until I had to.

To get there, I had to drive past landmarks that took me back to 1985—the county courthouse where the trials were held; the train station from which my mother traveled downtown to work; the DeKalb County police station at the intersection of Highway 285; the bypass loop around metro Atlanta—and make my way down Memorial Drive, a major east–west artery once named Fair Street. It originates in the middle of the city, Memorial, and winds east from downtown ending at Stone Mountain, the nation's largest monument to the Confederacy. A lasting metaphor for the white mind of the South, Stone Mountain rises out of the ground like the head of a submerged giant—the nostalgic dream of Southern heroism and gallantry emblazoned on its brow: in bas-relief, the enormous figures of Stonewall Jackson, Robert E. Lee, and Jefferson Davis. Not far from its base is the apartment we lived in that last year, at the 5400 block of Memorial, number 18-D.

Though I knew exactly where it was, knew the landmarks leading up to it, I drove right past at first and had to double back to enter the tree-lined front gate. From there I could see Stone Mountain in the distance, suddenly visible where Memorial crests, as if to remind me what is remembered here and what is not.

The last time I was at the apartment complex, the morning after her death, I could see the faded chalk outline of her body on the pavement, the yellow police tape still stuck to the door, the small, round hole in the wall beside her bed where a single bullet—a missed shot—had lodged. Nothing in the landscape today bears evidence to any of that, though everything seems to carry the imprint of loss. Row after row of rusted stair rails and window screens mark the shabby buildings—just a decade old when we moved in—and a lighter shade of paint coats the walls, as if to hide the dark history beneath it.

Standing under the window to what had been my mother's bedroom, I thought of the bullet hole: so small an imprint of the event that changed forever our lives. It would have been repaired soon after, filled and painted over, and I wondered now if the building had settled more with age, the walls shifting. I've seen the depression a once covered nail head can leave when a house settles, a pock in the drywall like a wound opening from beneath the surface. That's what's drawn me back: the hidden, covered over, nearly erased. I need now to make sense of our history, to understand the tragic course upon which my mother's life was set and the way my own life has been shaped by that legacy.

———

I KEEP AN IMAGE IN MY HEAD OF MYSELF FROM that first day after her death, at the apartment. There's a video recording of my arrival, made by a local news station, and so the image is not only of those few moments, but of watching myself—from a distance—entering my former life for what I thought to be the last time. In the footage I walk up the stairs to the door and step in, shutting it behind me. When I think of it now I don't hear any words, the volume on mute. Perhaps the reporter spoke our names; or perhaps she did not, calling my mother *victim* instead. And in my mind's eye a caption fills the bottom of the screen: it identifies me as *daughter of the murdered woman*. Even then I felt as though I were watching someone else—a young woman on the cusp of her life, adulthood and bereavement gripping her at once.

The young woman I'd become, walking out of that apartment hours later, was not the same one who went into it. It's as if she's still there, that girl I was, behind the closed door, locked in the footage where it ends. Often, I have seen that doorway in my dreams. Only now is it a threshold I can cross.

Thou art thy mother's glass, and she in thee
Calls back the lovely April of her prime
—SHAKESPEARE, SONNET 3

1.

ANOTHER COUNTRY

THERE IS A LARGE BIRTHMARK ON THE BACK OF my thigh. Even though it has been with me over half a century, I can't recall which leg bears its dark outline, and so I have to look at myself backward in a mirror to remember. Seeing it is not unlike encountering a forgotten scar, a remnant that recalls the moment of wounding. It takes me back to my early childhood: the long, warm days in Mississippi when I wore shorts much of the time and the birthmark was plainly visible, not hidden as it usually is now. Though not the shape of a hand, it is the size of one, and in exactly the spot where, if you were told to sit on your hands as my mother was, you might leave a mark.

Across cultures myths abound about the imprint a mother can make even before her child crosses the threshold into the world, the way her desires or fears can be

manifest on the body: birthmarks in the shape or color
of food she craved, a lock of gray hair where she tugged
at her own. To stanch the cravings, they say, eat a bit of
dirt or clay; to steady the hand that worries the hair, sit
on it. Had my mother done any of this, there might have
been a single story in my family about what my birthmark symbolizes. The only thing the elders agreed on
was that it looked like a place on a map, somewhere my
mother might have dreamed of but had never been. I've
often imagined her anticipating my arrival, both hopeful
and anxious about the world, the particular time and
place I would enter: a fierce longing taking shape inside her.

In the spring of 1966, when I was born, my mother
was a couple of months shy of her twenty-second birthday. My father was out of town, traveling for work, so
she made the short trip from my grandmother's house to
Gulfport Memorial Hospital, as planned, without him.
On her way to the segregated ward she could not help
but take in the tenor of the day, witnessing the barrage
of rebel flags lining the streets: private citizens, lawmak-
ers, Klansmen (often one and the same) raising them
in Gulfport and small towns all across Mississippi. The
twenty-sixth of April that year marked the hundredth
anniversary of Mississippi's celebration of Confederate
Memorial Day—a holiday glorifying the old South, the

Lost Cause, and white supremacy—and much of the fervor was a display, too, in opposition to recent advancements in the civil rights movement. She could not have missed the paradox of my birth on that particular day: a child of miscegenation, an interracial marriage still illegal in Mississippi and in as many as twenty other states.

Sequestered on the "colored" floor, my mother knew the country was changing, but slowly. She had come of age in the summer of 1965, turning twenty-one in the wake of Bloody Sunday, the Watts riots, and years of racially motivated murders in Mississippi. Unlike my father, who'd grown up a white boy in rural Nova Scotia, hunting and fishing, free to roam the open woods, my mother had come into being a black girl in the Deep South, hemmed in, bound to a world circumscribed by Jim Crow. Though my father believed in the idea of living dangerously, the necessity of taking risks, my mother had witnessed the necessity of dissembling, the art of making of one's face an inscrutable mask before whites who expected of blacks a servile deference. In the summer of 1955, when she was eleven years old, she'd seen what could happen to a black child in Mississippi who had not behaved as expected, stepping outside the confines of racial proscription: in my grandmother's copy of *Jet* magazine, Emmett Till's battered remains, his destroyed face.

EVEN HAD MY MOTHER WANTED TO IGNORE THE
racial violence and increasing turbulence around her, my
grandmother would not allow it. In her house the latest
issue of *Jet* lay on the coffee table beside a book of documentary photographs of the civil rights movement, images ranging from lynchings to peaceful protests and the
resilient faces of black Americans—constant reminders
of the necessity of fighting for justice in a state where the
external reminders were increasingly unavoidable. The
year before my mother met my father, the civil rights
activist Medgar Evers had been gunned down in his
driveway in Jackson. That year, 1963, my grandmother
joined a group of black citizens in the Biloxi wade-in to
protest being denied the right to use the public beaches.
To mourn Evers, the protesters placed hundreds of black
flags in the sand—an image my mother, watching from
the seawall, would not forget. Nor would she forget hearing the news of the three civil rights activists working on
the Freedom Summer campaign to register black voters
in Mississippi. James Chaney, Andrew Goodman, and
Michael Schwerner had been abducted and murdered in
June 1964, their bodies found two months later, buried
under the weight of an earthen berm in Neshoba County.
　　When the news reached her, my mother was out of

the state on a field trip with her college theater troupe. Back home the Ku Klux Klan had initiated its campaign of terror, the Mississippi she returned to having grown even more frightening. That summer was a season of fires, of danger coming ever closer: flaming crosses and black churches burning all around the state. My mother and grandmother, living across the street from a church, slept less soundly then, awakening often in the night to listen.

It was against that backdrop of imminence and upheaval that my parents, both college students at the time, fell in love. They met in a literature course on modern drama, and their conversations on books and theater propelled them from the classroom out into the afternoon sunlight as they walked the campus and beyond, among the rolling green hills of Kentucky. When they eloped in 1965, traveling across the Ohio River into Cincinnati, where it was legal for them to be married, only my mother fully understood what this might mean for me, the child she was already carrying. In letters to my father during their months apart, she was at once sanguine and practical, hopeful for a changing nation but also aware that any child she brought into the world would have much to learn in order to be safe. That meant I would need to understand the realities I would face: the painful, oppressive facts of a place slow to accept integration even as it was now the law of the land. My father, idealistic in nature, was still naive enough to believe I could grow up as free of the burdens of race—of blackness, that is—as he was.

They complemented each other, as opposites do: my mother graceful and reserved, attentive to details; my father, with his rough manners, rowdy and bookish at once, often distracted by his thoughts. It was my mother who stanched the blood on my cheek when, after watching my father shaving, I tried using his straight razor; it had been my father, absentminded, who'd left the razor on the counter within my reach. One day, when I cut my knee in the ditch outside, revealing what appeared to be a layer of white skin underneath, I lay between them, holding their hands up side by side, asking why they weren't the same color, why I didn't match either of them exactly. *What was I?* "You have the best of both worlds," they told me, not for the first time.

Out in the world, alone with either of them, I was just beginning to feel a profound sense of dislocation. If I was with my father, I measured the polite responses from white people, the way they addressed him as "Sir" or "Mister." Whereas my mother would be called "Gal," never "Miss" or "Ma'am," as I had been taught was proper. So different was the treatment I received with each of them that I was unsure where or how I belonged. Only at home, the three of us together, did I feel profoundly *theirs*, and in that trinity of mother, father, and child I would shut my eyes and fall asleep on the high bed between them.

OUTSIDE THAT BEDROOM WAS A LONG, NARROW hallway leading to the den and, just inside the door, a tall bookcase that held my attention countless afternoons. It housed my parents' books along with a set of encyclopedias my mother had insisted my grandmother purchase, instead of bronzing my baby shoes, to commemorate my birth. In the earliest dream I can recall, that hallway led to something unknown by which I was both drawn and vaguely frightened, a hint of danger that lay before me. In the dream I woke to a house so dark and quiet it seemed I was alone. I rose then and stood in the doorway, peering down the length of the hall. Opposite me, at the other end, blocking the bookcase, was a figure the size of a man: faceless and made entirely of the crushed shells that covered the driveway beside our house, the sharp edges I'd walked over barefoot countless times.

It makes sense to me now that my earliest recollected dream took on such a shape. By then my father was in graduate school part-time, working on his PhD in English, becoming a writer. Had I told him what frightened me, he might have reminded me, as a comfort, that the imagery resembled some of the stories he recited to me at bedtime: the trials of Odysseus, his encounter with the Cyclops blocking the exit to the cave; the monster Grendel, at the entrance to the mead hall, in the legend of Beowulf. Beyond those tales were the stories of Narcissus, Icarus, Cassandra, the riddle of the Sphinx—stories about bravery, vanity, hubris, knowledge.

I liked to curl up next to him in his large chair as he read. One evening, I ran my finger along his throat, over the knot there sharp as a knuckle.

"What's this, Daddy?" I asked. From Sunday school I knew the story of Adam and Eve, but not the part my father now recounted: how when Adam bit the apple from the tree of knowledge it lodged in his throat, giving to his descendants this lasting anatomical feature.

"Does it hurt?" I asked.

"No," he said, furrowing his brow as usual. "But it is one of the consequences of knowledge."

"Why don't *I* have one?"

"You do," he said, placing my hand against my own throat. "It's just smaller. Say something and you can feel it."

What my father wanted me to know about the world

he did not always say explicitly and so I listened intently to his stories, finding myself in the characters. When I swung too high on my swing set even though he warned me not to—nearly going backward over the crossbar, the chain buckling and sending me flailing to the ground—I heard the story of Icarus. When I played too long before the mirror imitating my mother at her toilette, enthralled by my own face, it would be the story of Narcissus.

In the short stories he was writing, fictionalized accounts of our lives, he named my character Cassandra, after the figure from Greek mythology. For my father, the myth of Cassandra had been just another way he sought to guide me toward what he thought I needed to know. In some versions, Cassandra's fate is that she is merely misunderstood—not unlike what my father imagined to be the obvious fate of a mixed-race child born in a place like Mississippi. "She was a prophet," he told me, "but no one would believe her." Over the years, though, this second naming would come to weigh heavily on me. It was as if, in giving me that name, he had given me not only the burden of foresight but also the notion of causation— that whatever it was, if I could imagine it, see it in my mind's eye, it would happen *because* I had envisioned it. As if I had willed it into being.

The language of allegory and metaphor undergirded our days. "How'd you like to have *that* ball to play with?"

my father said one afternoon, pointing to the red sun great in the sky.

"Don't be silly," said my mother. "You know she'd burn her hands."

Even then I knew something had passed between them, some difference in how they aimed to prepare me for the world. My father believed—as the poet Robert Frost cautioned—that one must have a thorough education in figurative language. "What I am pointing out," Frost wrote, "is that unless you are at home in the metaphor, unless you have had your proper poetical education in the metaphor, you are not safe anywhere. Because you are not at ease with figurative values: you don't know the metaphor in its strength and its weakness. . . . You are not safe in science; you are not safe in history." My mother, who'd majored in literature and theater in college, must have believed as well in the necessity of an education in metaphor, and yet she was the direct one, less interested in abstractions and figures of speech than in more practical lessons, admonishments about dangers I could not yet imagine.

I REMEMBER LONG WALKS WITH MY FATHER ALONG the railroad tracks, the sounds of poetry he'd recite as I picked flowers or blackberries for my mother. We'd gather pennies we had left for the trains to flatten and I'd walk with them clutched in my hands until my palms held the memory of every childhood scrape and cut, the familiar scent of blood. At home my mother would have corn pudding waiting for us, the kitchen warm and fragrant. On the windowsill the jar of flowers I'd picked caught the afternoon sun and held it like bottled light. Everything a marvel: crawfish building chimneys, pellet by pellet, above their burrows; machinery at the shipyard and the great locomotives lurching at the railroad switch; the rhythm of language and the power of words to alter what I saw.

"Look out the window," my father said. He had been entertaining me with a wolf hand puppet and the story of Little Red Riding Hood. "See that wolf out there?" he asked, pointing to my great-aunt Sugar, who was at that moment transformed: a wolf in a day dress and hat, walking upright through the woods behind our house. Even my mother, shelling peas at the kitchen sink, had looked outside and laughed. We were safe; nothing outside would harm us.

This was the place of my childhood wonder, of my parents' fleeting happiness, my unquestioning belief that my life would always be just as it was then, in the close arrangement of daily life with my mother's family. We lived with my grandmother, right next door to my aunt Sugar, on the small plot of land where my great-grandmother's house had stood; Eugenia McGee had borne seven children there, in a modest unpainted Victorian with a wraparound porch, long since razed. Only five of them survived to adulthood, and my grandmother was still a girl when Eugenia died, the land passing on to her and Sugar, the two remaining daughters. Their houses stood here now, just across the highway—what used to be a pasture—from the house their brother, my great-uncle Son, had built for his wife, Lizzie.

Surrounding us was a wider radius of people who'd grown up with my elders, many of them, like us, charting their family history back to when the small section of town called North Gulfport had been a settlement of former slaves. There was the community center, built by Mennonite missionaries, where I took swimming lessons; an Elks lodge where Uncle Son had been a member since the fifties; several churches and just as many small nightclubs and juke joints, including Son's Owl Club, where my mother, as a girl, had helped choose records for the jukebox, and where my grandmother had worked the kitchen on weekends making gumbo or red beans and rice. There was also a baseball field where Son's team played—my father as catcher, the only white player on the diamond.

Son was tall and handsome with a trim mustache above perfect teeth that he clenched when he spoke—as if there were always a cigar between them. He wore elegant lace-up shoes, finely ribbed undershirts, and creased trousers, even when he mowed his lawn. He was high yellow, so light he could nearly pass for white, and folks in the neighborhood whispered about his paternity, speculating that a white man called Mr. Griswold—for whom the community had originally been named—was actually his father, and had passed down through quitclaim deeds much of the land in North Gulfport on which Son's rental houses now stood.

His wife, Aunt Lizzie, was high yellow, too, a large woman with pillows of flesh into which I'd sink when she pulled me into her arms, her bosom fragrant and white with talc. In the fifties Son had built the nightclub right beside their house, so as not to be far from her when he worked. He parked his Cadillac in the driveway between the two. Unlike most other houses in the neighborhood, theirs was fully air-conditioned, and Aunt Lizzie kept it cold as a funeral parlor, the lace curtains drawn against the afternoon heat. A large Bible lay open on a reading stand beneath portraits of Jesus, Kennedy, and King. When Son sat with my father some evenings in the front room, the women in the back of the house laughing around the kitchen table, I would lie at his feet taking in the heady scent of his cigars, the glow of bourbon swirled in a cut crystal glass, and the sound of his voice, low and lilting.

Aunt Sugar's house was a squat bungalow of masonry brick, a bunker with jalousie windows—*jealousy* windows, she called them. "That wolf's just mad he can't get in my house." She'd had it built when she retired, returning to Gulfport when I was born, after twenty-five years in Chicago. Her first task had been to make sure my skull was perfectly formed, though not merely for beauty. Firmly believing that the right shape would facilitate the acquisition of knowledge, Sugar spent an hour every day massaging my head with oil as though she were a sculptor.

Born in 1906, Sugar was ten years older than my grandmother and had raised her and the younger children when their mother died, seeing to not only their education but also their spiritual enlightenment. Back when there was nothing but an arbor in which to congregate, she had started a church there, a congregation that, according to family legend, would one day become Mount Olive Baptist, just across the street from our small plot of land. Though she'd been married once, I grew up thinking of Sugar as a spinster—either no longer interested in men or simply unwilling to settle, as she put it, on one who "would not work," who was not her equal. "Never marry a man with less education than you," she told me again and again.

In the stories I heard about her, she was the family heroine, standing up to everyone, white people included, always ready with a sharp-tongued comeback to their routine terms of diminishment. Once, when she was still a young woman, a white man walking past the house called out to her, "Hey, Auntie"—the familiar term used then by whites to address any black woman. She didn't miss a beat with her reply—her shotgun propped just inside the door—"And now exactly when did my brother marry your mother?"

Sugar stood six feet tall, bone thin and wiry, her long fingers as suited to playing the piano in church as to crocheting lace. As soon as I was big enough to hold my own small fishing rod, she'd take me most weekends down to the pier at Gulfport to fish. We'd rise just before the sun came up on Saturday and meet in the yard between the two houses to gather worms. I'd hold the flashlight and watch as she dug a slender finger into the soft black dirt, pulling them out one by one. Out on the pier, we'd sit together in silence but for the sound of her humming. Every now and then she'd spit tobacco juice into a cup. To engender the patience I'd need for our fishing trips she taught me first to trap crawfish in the ditch that ran alongside the property. I'd learned to attach a piece of fat to the end of a string with a safety pin and drag it through the muddy water, watching intently even though I knew I would not be able to see what was waiting to strike.

Though Sugar's speech was different from my father's, it too was the language of idiom and metaphor. She'd hush me to a whisper in church, telling me to be "quiet as a rat pissing on cotton." Every secret began "quiet as it's kept." When she named her little dog Toby, after what she said was the hoodoo word for a charm of protection, I was delighted, certain she was magical, a shape-shifter. She loved the poetry of the Psalms, often chanting them as she went about her daily tasks. Many years later, when dementia kept her from speaking normally, she'd chant whatever she needed to say in that same cadence. Long before we recognized the signs of her disease for what they were, Sugar would appear each day at the back door, singing my name through the screen, her upturned palm holding out toward me three underripe figs: an offering. *Wait, be patient*, they seemed to say, *and sweetness will follow*. Without words, she was teaching me the figurative power of objects, their meaningful juxtapositions.

Together we gathered pecans when they dropped from the trees in the backyard, picked figs and persimmons before the birds could get to them, put away jars of preserves each season. Some days she'd pull out dusty medical books and show me the kinds of research and experiments she'd performed, working in a lab in Chicago. I'd linger over photographs of her in a white coat, bent over a Bunsen burner or inspecting test tubes. Her stories were filled with the excitement of discovery, and I imagined the secrets that could be unlocked by the mixing of different substances, the application of heat, the observations and revelations of a keen eye. In her parlor, science and divination merged. She read the signs, predicted fortune in the freckles on my skin: "Mole on the hand, that's money by the pan; mole on the neck, money by the peck . . ." Those afternoons passed deliciously slowly; at teatime she'd serve iced tea with butter sandwiches—the brown edges cut off and soaked in milk laced with sugar. All the days sweet like that.

DOWN THE STREET THE GULF AND SHIP ISLAND line ran north–south toward Jackson, beside Old Highway 49. Just a few yards from my grandmother's house, flanking her driveway, was the new Highway 49, a busy four-lane road stretching over what had been a pasture. At night I could hear the sound of a train going by from one direction, the long whistle as it met the crossing at the Four Corners, and on the other side the rumble of eighteen-wheelers that shook the ground and rattled our windows. Nestled between the two, our tiny patch of native geography seemed, to my child's eye, vast.

Though Son and Lizzie were separated from us by the highway, we could see their kitchen windows clearly enough and watched every morning for the blinds to be raised, the curtains opened—if only until late afternoon— a signal that all inside was well. Over the years, I spent my summer days skipping between those houses, sometimes having dinner and staying the night with Aunt Sugar or crossing Highway 49 to visit with my great-aunt and -uncle. My mother had grown up the only child among them, doing those same things, and she'd taught me how to announce my arrival at their houses: the coded knock that had been created for her—a quick rapping at Sugar's door—and the *Yoo-hoo* we called out, standing on the front stoop of Son and Lizzie's house. They doted on me, these elders, just as they had doted on her, and I loved the singular attention I received from each of them, the comfort of that small enclave of close relations.

There were few children my age in the neighborhood and I spent a lot of time alone. When not in my playroom or outside by myself I would sit quietly in the presence of adults, watching and listening. Often it was the women from my grandmother's church, the Ladies' Auxiliary Group, chanting the Lord's Prayer and discussing scripture. Most of all, I loved watching my mother. In the mornings before I left for school she'd be up early, sitting at the dresser, putting up her hair. On weekends I'd watch as she dressed to go out with my father in the evening. Tall and graceful, she'd wear pearl earrings that dangled from French wires or gold hoops that brushed her cheeks when she turned her head. Sometimes she'd wear a cameo nestled in the hollow of her throat, a black velvet choker holding it in place. The fine curl at the nape of her neck made her look even more delicate, as if no amount of armor could shield such a vulnerable spot.

WHEN I BEGAN TO GO OUT WITH BOTH MY PAR-ents, outside of the confines of North Gulfport to a store or the movie theater, I watched the ways white people responded to us. That my parents were beautiful would have been reason enough to stare, but in Mississippi, in the late sixties and early seventies, it had been only a few years since the beaches were integrated to comply with national law, and the schools were yet to be fully desegre-gated across the state. Ross Barnett, the former governor, was monitoring interracial activity, and my grandmother had been on the list of people to watch ever since she'd tried to place my parents' 1965 wedding announcement in the local newspaper. Separation of the races was still the way of things, maintained by custom if not upheld by law, and my parents and I met with a great deal of hostility most places we went.

I could see it on the faces of the white people we encountered—how even the nicer ones just shook their heads, whispering, *Such a cute little thing; too bad she's black*; how others stared at us, sucking their teeth. Sometimes this hostility turned to outright intimidation: someone following us out of Woolworth's to the car, my mother gripping my father's arm to prevent him turning around and engaging the man behind us; someone else driving slowly by the house, glaring at us as we sat on the front porch; a group of three or four men accosting my father on his way home from work on the docks, asking: *What's wrong with you? Why you living among the niggers?*

My mother and grandmother, having lived with this kind of attention, were accustomed to scrutiny and intimidation: a stream of headlights searching the front windows of the house at night, the sexually charged calls from white men driving by in broad daylight. In the late fifties and early sixties my grandmother had given shelter to several Mennonite missionaries who came to North Gulfport to teach, repair the dilapidated housing of the very poor, and minister to the community. For weeks at a time these young white missionaries would stay at her house, and it wasn't long before their presence and the work they were doing was noticed by local whites. First there was a bomb threat, directed at the Bible camp where the Mennonites were believed to be promoting integration, the camp my mother attended. Then, the Ku Klux Klan threatened to bomb the Mount Olive Baptist Church across the street. Undeterred, my grandmother began to sleep with a pistol beneath her pillow. In spite of the danger, she was adamant in her belief that she must do this work, must open her doors to help. "A moral obligation," she called it.

Though my mother and my grandmother met all of this with a similar stoicism, they responded differently. My mother was averse to guns, to confrontation; whereas my grandmother saw guns as a necessity, telling me countless times the way to confront a would-be intruder: "First fire a warning shot," she said, "and if they keep coming, aim at the legs, shoot to wound."

Those words marked my first awareness that any danger we might face was not limited to the world outside our close-knit community, the radius of those houses, but could come right to us, right up into the yard, perhaps even the front door. Though I was too young to recall the night the Klan burned a cross in our driveway, I heard the story again and again, and the night lives in my memory as experience. I see it as though watching

a scene in a documentary, silent but for the metal box
fan in the window, a whirring sound like an old movie
projector:

   *The men arrive late in the evening, long after supper:
my parents still sitting together in the den, watching television; my grandmother and my uncle Charlie in the kitchen,
washing the last of the dishes. All of them dead now, I see
them moving through the house like ghosts. Even I am a
ghost in this story—an infant self of whom I have no recollection, my inscrutable face still white as my father's. My
grandmother peers through the blinds at the group of them—
seven or eight men in white robes carrying a man-size cross;
in the bedroom my mother watches over me, the blackout
curtains drawn, all the lights in the house extinguished so
that, but for the faint glow of a hurricane lamp in the corner, we are all in darkness; my father and uncle, rifles in
hand, waiting silently in the front room as, outside, the fire
ignites.*

   In my grandmother's house the act of remembering,
recounting that story, was meant to ensure my future
safety, protection gained through knowledge and the
vigilance it brings, a certain hyperawareness: hair rising
on the back of my neck when I'd hear a particular kind
of southern accent, a tensing in my spine when I'd see
the Confederate flag or the gun rack on a truck following
us too closely down the road.

WITHIN THE TIGHT CIRCLE OF EXTENDED FAMILY, with their watchful interventions into my daily life, I felt protected, insulated from racial intimidation and violence, regardless of the ferment all around us. Uncle Son drove the school bus for the Mississippi Head Start program, picking me up first in the morning and dropping me off last each afternoon so I could keep him company on the route. My mother worked for Head Start, too, in administration, and her office was right next to the Catholic church where I attended class. My grandmother had quit her job at the drapery factory downtown the day I came home from the hospital and had been working at home as a seamstress since then, her great cutting table and sewing machines in the room just next to my playroom, so she could watch over me while my parents were still at work.

Sometimes after school I'd lie beneath the cutting table on its wide shelf, curled up among the remnants of fabric, listening along to her radio programs: *Ellery Queen*, *Dark Shadows*—what I realize now must have been an audio rebroadcast of the popular television show. She'd tell me stories about her life as a young woman, answering questions about my absent grandfather with a seeming matter-of-factness. In one story about leaving home

for the first time, traveling north in Mississippi with her
new husband, my grandmother described what she saw
from the car window: "On either side of the road, fields
of white gladioluses." I understand the quiet naïveté of it
now, and the sadness of it, too: never having seen cotton
growing, she mistook the plants that had come to mean
the back-bending labor of slaves and sharecroppers for
the flowers that symbolize honor and remembrance, the
swords of gladiators, tall borders of pleasure gardens. She
did not know, at that moment, the truth of her marriage.
On that journey, she'd tell me, nothing turned out to be
as it first appeared. In my childhood full of the lessons
of mythology and cautionary tales, this was yet another.

THAT SO MANY OF MY RELATIVES WERE AROUND
me made the routine absences of my father less pronounced. It was part of the natural order of things that
he would be gone for some time, following which I'd see
him for a while before he departed again. A year after I
was born he had taken a commission as an officer in the
Royal Canadian Navy and, after his initial training in
British Columbia, spent most of 1967 and part of 1968 on
a destroyer, the *Centennial*, cruising around the world to
commemorate Canada's one hundredth anniversary. One

of the few photographs I have of the three of us together is a formal portrait taken in 1969 in my grandmother's den. It was the last photograph we'd take together as a family—my father sitting on a wooden armchair, my mother balanced on the arm, her long legs crossed, and me between them, puckish in a green dress. I see in that photograph now my grandmother's desire for commemoration. Most pictures we had were snapshots taken casually, but for this one my grandmother had called in a photographer. Two years after the Supreme Court had ruled, in *Loving v. Virginia*, that laws prohibiting interracial marriage were unconstitutional, it was as if she wanted the formality of a professional portrait to make visible the legitimacy of my parents' union, our family, in a place where we were still seen as an aberration.

The photographer who came to take the portrait was a double amputee. Though my mother warned me not to stare at him, I could not resist finding a way to steal glances at the space just below his knees where his shins would have been. When he scratched the air around one of the missing limbs I was watching him with such intense curiosity that he caught me. He must have been accustomed to the rough curiosity of children. Leaning toward me, he spoke barely above a whisper. "I can still feel it," he said, "even though it's gone." In the photograph you can see my mother pressing my arm with her

forefinger as if to make visible her imprint on me. I am
looking directly at the photographer, toward a new idea
of absence, of phantom ache—knowing nothing about
how potently one might come to feel it.

MY FATHER HAD A DIFFERENT KIND OF COMMEMO-
ration in mind. In the aftermath of the *Loving* decision,
he'd wanted to take a trip someplace where our color
differences might be less noticeable, where my mother
might be able to relax. Ignoring her qualms about the
dangers of a long journey, over a thousand miles, my
father bought a used Lincoln Continental to get us to
Mexico. I have a vague recollection of the seemingly end-
less stretch of blacktop, how that long car seemed to float
above it as I dozed on the back seat. The sun hung low
and heavy as we drove toward it. We were still three years
from the end of their marriage, but the best of our days
together already lay behind us in the darkening distance.
    What has stayed with me vividly from that trip, in-
scribed in the way that traumatic events draw a map of
connections in the brain, is my near drowning in the hotel
pool. My father was always reading, and so I imagine
he must have gone inside to retrieve a book, leaving my
mother poolside as I splashed in the shallow end. I don't

recall how I ended up in the deeper section. For what seemed a long moment I was suspended there, looking up through a ceiling of water, the high sun barely visible overhead. I don't recall being afraid as I sank, only that I was enthralled by what I could see through that strange and wavering lens: my mother, who could not swim, leaning over the edge—arms outstretched—reaching for me. She was in the line of the sun and what she did not block radiated around her head, her face like an annular eclipse, dark and ringed with light.

I have just one photograph as a record of our journey. In it I am alone. There are mountains in the distance behind me and I am sitting on a mule. On the back, in my father's elegant script: "Tasha, Monterrey 1969." Of all the photographs of my early childhood, this one—I can see it now—shows me what each of my parents, in different ways, needed me to know. It was my father's idea to place me on the back of the mule—my father who, perhaps oblivious to his own metaphors of animal husbandry, had referred to me in one of his poems as a *crossbreed*. The photograph was perhaps his version of a linguistic joke: the sight gag of a mixed-race child riding her namesake, animal origin of the word *mulatto*.

My mother, knowing very well what the visual metaphor meant, could not have thought it was funny. They would have agreed only that I needed to understand it:

You are not safe in science; you are not safe in history. Whatever hope she'd had early on, when they were first in love
and thinking that love might be enough to counter the
challenges of racism I would face, the country had by then
shown her otherwise: that love alone would not protect
me. She knew that as a mixed-race child—halfway between them—I would ultimately be alone in the journey
toward an understanding of self, my place in the world,
yet carrying the invisible burdens of history, borne on the
back of metaphor. She knew, too, that language would
be used to name and thereby attempt to constrain me—
mongrel, mulatto, half-breed, nigger—and that, as on the
back of the mule, I would be both bound to and propelled
by it. My mother wanted only that I not be destroyed by it.

AFTER THE TRIP TO MEXICO MY FATHER BEGAN HIS
graduate studies full-time, and so he was away from us
during the week, in New Orleans, staying in an apartment he shared with another graduate student. Though I
missed him, turning my longing for him into petulance
with my mother, I looked to her with the focus of an
only child with but one parent—at turns possessive and
then withdrawn, as if by withholding some affection I
might garner more of it from her.

On weekends my parents would take turns making the drive to visit. The trip from Gulfport was just over an hour, and though we'd done it many times, my mother never quite learned her way into the city from the highway. She'd pull off I-10 at Vieux Carré and my father would be waiting for us at the end of the ramp. I'd see him there holding out his thumb, pretending to hitchhike, and for a moment it was as though he were a stranger, someone my mother was stopping to help in a place she knew little about. If she felt any pull to the place of her birth—any familiarity or longing—she never mentioned it. Sometimes I think that's where her silence began, as if she'd locked away in a box, within the confines of a place whose name means "Old Square," a past she was too hurt by or ashamed of to pass down to me.

THIS IS WHAT I KNOW: GWENDOLYN ANN TURN-bough was born in New Orleans in 1944. When she arrived in June of that year, my grandmother was almost thirty, studying at a beauty school to be a hairdresser and living in the French Quarter to be near the port from which her husband, Ralph, had shipped off with his naval unit. In my grandmother's telling, her labor began before the doctor could get there, and so she gave birth to my mother by herself. For thirty minutes, she lay side by side with the newborn, the umbilical cord still joining them, until the doctor arrived and severed it. Long after my mother was dead, my grandmother still described the ache she felt at her navel: phantom pain in the place that once joined them.

The rest of the story carries its own omen. My grandfather had departed just two days before my mother was born, and within a week, his mother Narcissus traveled from Mississippi to New Orleans to verify the newborn's paternity. Here, too, the character of Narcissus enters our family mythology—this time as a vain and color-struck woman who looked white and could not believe her son had married someone as dark as my grandmother. Narcissus Turnbough wanted to see herself reflected in my mother's face. She wanted also to see if my mother had what she believed to be a particular family trait: a red birthmark at the base of the head that she had passed to each of her children. My mother did indeed bear the mark, but rather than be convinced of the indelible link between them, Narcissus took one look at my brown-skinned mother, then turned and left.

Despite that rejection, it seemed at first that my mother had been born into a happy union: a doting mother, an anxious father at sea awaiting news. In the photograph of mother and child taken not long after, my grandmother is smiling her wide smile, her teeth white and perfectly straight. She's seated outside in a wicker chair, holding the swaddled baby up, pressed to her face—a gesture full of happiness. But the photograph hints, too, at another story. I can see it in the tall grass brushing her ankles, the blades bent as if moved by wind. I can hear the folk warning, as if a whisper from the frame in a knowing voice: *Don't let the grass grow under your feet.* Nearly a year after my mother's birth, my grandmother learned Ralph had taken another wife. By then there was nothing for her to do but file for divorce, pack her things, and ride the train back home to Mississippi, my mother on her lap. Had my grandmother read the signs, she might have seen this coming, might have known earlier that things were not as they seemed. Her marriage ended as it began, with a journey and windows out of which she watched the world go by.

My mother saw her father just once after that. According to my grandmother, at age sixteen my mother decided she needed to meet him—perhaps to ask why he'd done what he'd done. He was living in California by then, still married to the woman with whom he'd committed bigamy, and my grandmother arranged for my mother to take the train to Los Angeles by herself. She was gone just over a week, and when she returned my mother did not speak of him again, neither to her mother nor to me.

I grew up knowing this story, knowing that my

mother's life had begun with abandonment, that she had revisited it on that journey, and that she'd grown up with a constant reminder: my grandmother kept a portrait of Ralph Turnbough behind the door at the end of the long hallway in her house, a charcoal drawing done by a street artist in the French Quarter at Jackson Square. In it my grandfather wears his US Navy uniform. He is devastatingly handsome—high cheekbones, a chiseled jaw, and full lips—features I recognize as my mother's. Perhaps it was because of that resemblance that my grandmother could never get rid of the portrait. Though she kept the portrait just out of sight, it was still there—his absence haunting the house as if to betray his wife and daughter every day. Whenever I passed through the doorway in the hall on my way to the bookcase, there at the threshold I'd seen in my dream, I'd be reminded, too.

IN NEW ORLEANS MY MOTHER AND I RARELY WENT out alone, though occasionally she'd take me shopping downtown while my father was working in his office on campus or in the library. We'd take the streetcar, ride it all the way down Saint Charles Avenue from my father's uptown apartment near Tulane University. My mother loved the big houses along Saint Charles, their white

columns and verandas set back behind verdant shrubs
and bright bougainvillea, wrought-iron fences crowned
by black fleurs-de-lis. As we rode, she'd occasionally look
up from whatever novel she was reading to point out her
favorites. I'd marvel at the eternal flames of the flickering
gas lamps, the graceful iron cages that held them behind
glass, and wonder about the lives of the people inside
such elegant houses.

Downtown we never ventured into the Quarter but
spent hours in the department stores along Canal Street:
Maison Blanche, Godchaux's, D. H. Holmes. My mother
would study the displays of dresses, then we'd walk down
Canal to a notions store for a pattern, Vogue or Butter-
ick, to make a dress or suit at home. Her closet was filled
with clothes that she and my grandmother had sewn,
and I loved the feel of them, how they held a trace of her
perfume. Often, playing hide-and-seek with my father,
I'd huddle in the closet, breathing in the earthy scent of
wool and lavender sachets.

While she was laying out the patterns, pinning them
to the fabric and cutting their outlines with pinking
shears, I'd go out by myself exploring the neighborhood
around my father's apartment: the cracked and buckled
sidewalks, the exposed roots of ancient live oaks, the drip
of window-unit air conditioners, the damp smell of moss
clinging to stone pavers across which I'd read the fading

signatures of slugs. One afternoon, just a street over, I came upon a group of children not much older than I was. They were having a birthday party and as I walked by slowly, hoping they might invite me into the yard to play, one of the larger boys pointed at me and yelled, "Zebra! Get her!" He was the first one to reach me where I stood, and when he shoved me, I pushed him to the ground and ran. They chased me then, all ten or so of them, all the way to the end of the block.

I had not heard that word before in relation to myself—*zebra*—and as I sat on the steps of my father's apartment teasing out the metaphor, I decided not to tell my parents what had happened. Did I think I was protecting them? Or was it something else that prompted my silence? I did not feel sorry for myself—I'd fought back—but I knew somehow that I must bear this knowledge alone.

For as long as I can remember, my father had been telling me that one day I would have to become a writer, that because of the nature of my experience I would have something necessary to say. When I look back on that moment, it seems the first inkling of my understanding at least part of what he must have meant. I sat there a long time, my eyes trained on a single black slug curved on the pavement before me, like a comma.

I DON'T KNOW HOW LONG AFTER IT WAS THAT WE began to make the trip to New Orleans to see my father less and less. It seems to me now that my parents were visiting each other mostly for *my* benefit, trying perhaps to prepare me for their impending separation and divorce. *You have the best of both worlds*, they tried to reassure me, and this permanent separation meant I would have two parental households, *two* places to call home. During one of our last visits my father drew a picture: It showed a not-to-scale map of the route between New Orleans, Mississippi, and Atlanta, with arrows pointing up and down the road, forming the cycle of travel that would come to define our lives as father and daughter. At the bottom was his address, and beside it, the hands and tiny round head of a cartoon person, only his eyes and the top half of his face visible—as if peering over the edge of the map to look for my location. Each time my father sent me a letter the little man would be there, a surrogate, somewhere on the page.

It took me a long time to realize how fully I had accepted my parents' narrative of my situation, their determined reassurances. For most of my life I have told myself that this separation didn't trouble me, that even then I was fine with it. I see now this was only the first of many stories I needed to tell myself over the years.

One of the last photographs from that time is a picture of me with my mother, taken a year before we left Mississippi. Perhaps my father is there, behind the camera. Perhaps he is not. In the picture, my mother and I are both dressed in purple: her paisley dress, my velvet frock. She's just begun to wear her hair in an Afro, a reddish corona around her head. We are in the living room at my grandmother's house and she is seated on a large, upholstered chair. I am standing close, leaning into her shoulder, our faces nearly touching. Tilting her head, she looks at me adoringly and I am smiling, demure, casting my eyes away from her. A heart locket dangles from the collar of my dress: "The shape of your face," she'd say, cradling my face in her hands.

There's a flaw in the picture, a white spot at the center of her face from which she already seems to be disappearing. If you were to multiply that spot, double its size every year for twelve years—beginning with our arrival in Atlanta—by the end of that time she'd be completely gone: only the space where she had been would remain, a hole like the shape of her Afro, or the sun.

2.

TERMINUS

FOR A LONG TIME I TRIED TO FORGET AS MUCH AS I could of the twelve years between 1973 and 1985. I wanted to banish that part of my past, an act of self-creation by which I sought to be made only of what I consciously chose to remember. I chose to mark the calendar year just after my mother and I left Mississippi as *ending*, and the moment of loss—her death—as *beginning*.

Those two years would be like the set of bookends I'd kept on my desk back then: two small globes, imprinted with a sepia map of the world, bracketing a few favorite volumes—*Wuthering Heights, The Great Gatsby, Light in August*. In my attempt at willed forgetting, I would collapse the distance between bookends, the year that ended the world of my happy early childhood pressing right up against the new world I'd entered suddenly as a motherless child. The years 1973 and 1985, side by side, with no books between them, no pages upon which the story I could not bear to remember had been written. But there is a danger in willed forgetting; too much can be lost. It's been harder for me to call back my mother when I have needed to most.

Of course, we're made up of what we've forgotten too, what we've tried to bury or suppress. Some forgetting is necessary and the mind works to shield us from things that are too painful; even so, some aspect of trauma lives on in the body, from which it can reemerge unexpectedly. Even when I was trying to bury the past, there were moments from those lost years that kept coming back, rising to mind unbidden. Those memories—some intrusive, some lovely—seem now to have a grander significance, like signposts on a path. It's a path I can see now only because I have followed it backward, attempting to find a moment of revelation, evidence of something being set in motion. There's a scene like that from the first few months after my mother and I moved to Atlanta:

It is winter, early evening, and I am watching as she changes out of the clothes she's worn to class and dresses for work. I can see her from the space that is my room, a closet off her bedroom barely large enough to hold my twin bed. The daffodils I picked for her on the way home from school are doubled in the mirror on her dresser. I watch her as the sky goes dark, streetlamps just coming on outside the small window above me. There must be someone else in the apartment, someone there to watch over me while she is gone, but I don't remember that part. I know only that I will sleep and in the morning she will be there again. So I stay awake until she leaves, wearing the uniform required for her job as a cocktail waitress in Underground Atlanta: black leotard and jeans, a heavy brass bullet belt slung low around her slender hips. I see it so clearly now, my young mother bending to kiss me, the bullets' cold metal brushing my hand, her body ringed in the objects of her undoing.

IN THE LATE SUMMER OF 1972 MY MOTHER AND I left Mississippi for good. I watched the pine woods slide by our window as she sang along with the radio. In my recollection it is always the same song, the Temptations' "Just My Imagination," though I know that can't be right. The song had debuted in 1971 and would have been played less frequently, certainly not over and over in the course of a daylong trip. I had watched her sing it so many times before we left, swaying over the ironing board as the afternoon sun backlit her, that even now I place her in the same moment—just as she kept setting the needle on the record player again and again. It's one of the few images I have in which she seems fully alive, without the pall that hangs over her in most other memories, the veil through which I can't help but see everything. It's as if what was to come was already laid out before us, that our fate lay in the geography toward which we were blithely driving.

My mother had been thinking of getting out of Mississippi for some time, long before I was born. In letters to the man who would become my father she lamented her desire to leave when there was so much work to be done to improve race relations and opportunities for blacks in the state. "I want to get out of this place," she wrote, "but I know my state needs me." By the end of the summer of 1964, my mother's desire to move to a better place must have begun to outpace her will to stay. For her, it had been eye-opening to be out of Mississippi, watching some of the events of those months from afar in larger towns around the South. On the back of a postcard, a photograph of the city skyline lit up against the night, she penned a note to my father: "Atlanta is interesting," she wrote. "Remind me to tell you about it. . . ."

It's no wonder that she'd be drawn to the city that epitomized the emergence of the New South. During the civil rights era Atlanta would garner a reputation for being racially progressive, and in the aftermath of the tumultuous 1960s it would be nicknamed by city leaders— without irony—"the City Too Busy to Hate." Long before that, however, it had another name: Founded in 1837, Atlanta began as "the end of the line." The proposed meeting point of the railroads, it was originally called Terminus.

I recall the moment we reached it. The drive had taken all day; the trunk of the car, loaded down with all our belongings, nearly dragging on the pavement. As we reached the outskirts of the city on Interstate 20, the skyline of Atlanta seemed to rise suddenly above the trees. In the angled light of late afternoon, it seemed two-dimensional, a dark cutout against the bright sky. If my mother saw some version of the idealized imagery of a postcard, this is the point at which our narratives of the journey diverge. In a letter to my father her account was upbeat: "The trip went well," she wrote, "only eight hours." Nothing more. But in my recollection the trip was not at all the easy passage she describes. Instead, I am haunted by a memory of smoke billowing from the hood of the car toward the skyline. I know this happened, but when? Perhaps the trauma of those years has made me collapse time and conflate the events of the weeks following our arrival with the very day of it. Or perhaps, as she often did, my mother hid the truth of her circumstances. In this case I can imagine the reason: My father had always hounded her about car maintenance, about changing the oil and keeping up the fluid levels. She would not have wanted him to know if she had not taken proper care, especially before setting out with me on a long trip.

This is what has stayed with me: my mother shutting off the engine, gripping the wheel tightly and letting the car coast to the side of the highway. As we stopped, I saw her cross herself, her lips silently moving. It was a gesture familiar to me—I had seen the nuns at Head Start perform it—but I did not know why my mother, who had been raised in the Baptist church, did it then. It would be more than a decade before I learned she had converted to Catholicism, though, over the years, I would see her make the sign of the cross frequently: a gesture I'd come to think of as more talisman than prayer.

For what seemed a long time we stood against the guardrail, waiting for help to arrive. My mother held me close to her, cars speeding by us. She was wearing the lime-green jumpsuit that I loved: short pants and a wide belt cinched at her tiny waist. It made her look like the heroine in a comic book—a cross between Wonder Woman and Lois Lane, amazon avenger and brainy career girl in love with the idea of a superman who would swoop down and save the day. I clung to her then, pressing my cheek against the ribbed fabric and tilting my head up toward the city on its distant, hilly terrain. As the smoke rose from the car toward the skyline, I couldn't help thinking that, at any moment, everything we had would be consumed by flames.

PERHAPS THAT'S THE TRICK THE MIND PLAYS IN grappling to make meaning of events of the past, to find a narrative thread, to read—looking back—the signs we did not pay attention to in the moment. In the days before we left Mississippi I had wept frequently, wishing silently that we would not go, that something would happen to change our plans and that we'd stay with my grandmother, in the close proximity of my father and extended family. Now, watching the tow truck driver with his fire extinguisher and seeing my mother's agitation, I felt vaguely responsible for our predicament, as though my behavior had jinxed us.

I was already a superstitious child: avoiding cracks in the sidewalk; sidestepping the broom so that it wouldn't touch my feet as my grandmother swept; spitting on it if it did; throwing salt over my shoulder at Aunt Sugar's table when I spilled it; uttering certain phrases to counteract the bad luck sure to follow some intentional act or—worse—to be brought on by something I'd inadvertently done; all of it, Aunt Sugar said, "keeping the devil at bay." I was mildly obsessive, too, in the way that many children are. My toys had to be perfectly arranged, all precise angles and even spacing. So meticulous was I about their placement that I could tell if they had been moved. From the moment I learned to tie my shoes I was obsessed with symmetry, that the laces be exactly the same in their tightness. Sometimes, I'd tie them over and over just to get it right. Already I had begun to feel that this at least was something I could control.

There is a belief among cognitive theorists that normal intrusive thoughts, when misinterpreted, can lead to obsessions and compulsive behavior, and that perhaps there is a link among those behaviors, childhood superstitions, and environmental factors: traumas like divorce, moving, the loss of a loved one. I do not know the moment that my normal childhood superstition gave way to something more consuming. More likely it was not a single moment but cumulative, escalating perhaps in those first tense minutes roadside in a strange city, my anxiety leading to misinterpretation: the idea of causality. As I stood clinging to my mother, I raised two fingers to my face and traced down from my forehead the outline of my nose and mouth—over and over to get it right, balanced, the pressure applied to either side in perfect symmetry. When my mother crossed herself at the arrival of the tow truck, my gesture must have looked like a flawed imitation of hers.

THE ATLANTA INTO WHICH WE'D ARRIVED WAS A
city in the midst of dramatic demographic, social, and
political change. Just over a decade before, the schools
had been officially desegregated. The physical barricades
that had been erected in southwest Atlanta to prevent
blacks from moving into white neighborhoods were, by
court order, removed, and what had been a gradual flight
of white residents to the surrounding suburbs had rapidly increased. In 1960 blacks had made up less than a
third of the city's residents, but by 1970 they represented
more than half of the population. In a previously white
enclave my mother found an apartment for us: a duplex
not far from the new school I would attend, Venetian
Hills Elementary.

A photograph of the seventh-grade class of 1962
shows nothing but white faces. By the fall of 1972, when
I entered first grade, there wasn't a single white student
in my class, and I don't recall seeing any in the rest of the
school. Most of the teachers were black but for a handful of whites who had not left for jobs in the suburbs.
Those who'd stayed, along with the newly hired black
teachers, embraced the racial transformation in the student body by adopting a curriculum that included the
history and cultural contributions of African Americans

year-round, not just during Black History Month. Only
the textbooks, the Dick and Jane readers left over from
the decade before the school desegregated, showed a version of the world that did not include black characters.

The walls of Venetian Hills were adorned with the
faces of black men and women of distinction: Ida B.
Wells, James Weldon Johnson, Langston Hughes, Mary
McLeod Bethune. Each day, after we had practiced writing, forming the letters in our ruled tablets, we reveled in
their stories. We sang of John Henry swinging his hammer, followed our teacher in the recitation of Dunbar's
dialect poems, performed Johnson's "The Creation," act-
ing it out with our hands: *And the light that was left from
making the sun / God gathered it up in a shining ball / And
flung it against the darkness, / Spangling the night with the
moon and stars.* It was as though another group of an-
cestors, however distant, surrounded me during school,
and in their afterglow my classmates and I were insulated
from everyday reminders of attitudes held by white people
who had left the neighborhood rather than live and send
their children to school alongside us. At assemblies, our
teachers led us in singing "Lift Every Voice and Sing," the
black national anthem, with as much fervor as we sang
the "Star-Spangled Banner," our hands over our hearts.

The school was the first place I began to feel at home.
I could walk to and from the school bus stop by myself

and, in the afternoons, I'd skip slowly along daydreaming and picking the flowers that grew along the sidewalk, black-eyed Susans or yellow and white daffodils,
my mother back at the apartment waiting for me. Things
were not so different from how they'd been in Mississippi
when my father was away at school during the week: the
two of us out in the world by ourselves.

Still, being in this new place was hard to get used to
and I slept fitfully. The two-story apartment seemed huge
and empty. On the ground floor, behind the long stair-
way, was a hollow space that, at night, looked like the
entrance to a cave. It was enough to heighten the childhood fears I'd begun to cultivate before we left Mississippi, fears that always involved some frightening figure
that might emerge from the shadows. My friend Dede
and I had been afraid to look too long into the recesses
of my grandmother's deep closet, so we had entertained
ourselves by telling stories about what lurked there. She
would recount how the devil took people to hell, how
the ground would open and he'd pull you in by your
ankles, or how you might go through a door you weren't
supposed to and find yourself there. We played Bloody
Mary, too, closing the blackout shades to make the room
dark as night in the middle of the day. Standing before a
mirror we'd take turns trying to summon her, saying her
name three times so that she would appear, reflected in

the glass. We'd have barely uttered the last syllable before one of us would call for Saint Christopher to protect us, the other yanking open the shades and flooding the room with light, to banish whatever it was we had summoned.

Now, away from the safety of my grandmother's house, I could not so easily banish what frightened me. If I had to go to the bathroom at night, I'd keep my eyes closed so that I would not see the mirror on my mother's dresser in the dark, afraid of what I'd find there. Nor would I go down to the kitchen for a glass of water, fearing that I might see what lurked in that space beneath the stairs.

My mother was determined to help me adjust to our lives in this new place, to be happy. One afternoon she had the idea of decorating the space beneath the stairs to make a playroom for me. Instead of trying to brighten it, we would make *use* of the darkness—like the night mind at work: a place of dreams, creative and fertile. We found everything we needed at the thrift store: a wide bolt of black velvet, enough yards to drape the whole ceiling and the opening to the narrow space. We made stars from cardboard and aluminum foil, planets out of Styrofoam balls flecked with glitter to catch even the smallest amount of light. Above the doorway she hung a sign: NATASHA'S ROOM BENEATH THE STARS.

I had a small table and chair, a lamp, and a shelf that held my books and all of my sacred objects: a thimble,

a pair of wooden spools, the hand-painted silk fan my
grandmother had used in church. The morning we left
Mississippi she'd put them all in one of Uncle Son's old
cigar boxes. "You're an easy child to love," she'd said,
drawing me close to her and wiping my face of tears.
Whenever I opened the box in the little space the air
would be filled with a familiar scent, and I'd sit there
conjuring every inch of my grandmother's house in my
mind's eye. I had begun to do this at school too, during
recess, with any group of children who would listen. It
began as a comfort, my rehearsing the memory of the
home we'd left. I'd call it up day after day, the exact
order of things in each room, the yard and ditch surrounding the house, and describe them in vivid detail.
Perhaps this is why that part of my memory exists for
me more fully than most of my days that first year: I was
already beginning to put into words what I thought then
I needed to keep from losing.

NOT LONG AFTER WE'D ARRIVED I HAD A HORRIBLE
dream: I was back at my grandmother's house, outside
in the yard, when the ground began to shake. Looking
down, I could see the earth splitting open, a deep chasm
over which I was standing, one foot on either side as it

widened. When I woke, I tried replacing the troubling images with happy ones as my mother had taught me to do.
I pictured flowers and candy, bright and colorful. I said
the words *daffodil* and *lollipop* over and over until their
meanings gave way to pure sound. Alone in the dark I
lulled myself back to sleep, listening to the rhythm of my
mother's breathing in the next room until it matched
my own.

We spent most of our time together—days she'd sit
with her books on the stoop and watch me as I played
hopscotch or rode my bicycle up and down the sidewalk
in front of our apartment. Every Saturday we'd go on
outings, most often to the public library where the pale
blue card with my name printed on it was a currency
worth more than gold. My mother would work in a car-
rel while I roamed the children's section, entertaining
myself for hours. After I'd checked out as many books
as I was allowed, I'd lie on the floor between the stacks,
reading, until it was time for us to go. Our apartment
wasn't air-conditioned, so the library was a respite from
the heat in the days of Indian summer.

One weekend when the weather was cooler she took
me to the zoo at Grant Park. The star attraction was Wil-
lie B., a great silverback gorilla who'd been in captivity
for years. My mother barely stopped to glance at him as
I lingered at the cage trying to intuit his thoughts. He sat

on his haunches, immovable as the Sphinx, and looked back morosely at the few people gathered before him, a small television his only companion, flickering in the background.

"Is he sad?" I asked, catching up to her.

"Wouldn't *you* be," she said, "isolated and alone like that?" There was something in her tone I could not understand, so I began my usual dialectic.

"But why?" I asked.

"What do you mean 'why'?"

"Why is he alone?"

"Because he's in a cage."

"But why is he in a cage?"

She looked away for a long moment then turned back to me, her eyes narrowed against the bright sunlight. "So you can come here and see him," she said.

"But why?" I said again, not quite sure what I was asking, what it was I wanted to know.

"We're not playing that game right now, Natasha," my mother said, exasperated, grabbing my hand and turning to go. She grew quiet then, brooding, and I knew that I had somehow disappointed her.

I could measure my days in two columns: those in which I had done something to please her, a mirror to her loveliness, days when she called me "sugar plum" and held my face in her hands; and, in the other column, all the

times I had done something that saddened or hurt or frus-
trated her. I remember her grabbing my hand the same
way another weekend at the movie theater. We'd been
watching a matinee about World War II, and toward the
end there was a scene in which the soldiers, fighting in
the trenches, showed great tenderness toward each other,
the wounded and dying. I had been caught up in it, the
camaraderie of shared experience, the heightened emotion
and imagery of solidarity among the men. The casualties
of the Vietnam War and the racism faced by black soldiers
returning home hardly registered in my consciousness.
Wistful, I had blurted out "I hope there's a war when *I*
grow up." She'd stood up swiftly then, taking my hand
and nearly dragging me up the aisle as the credits rolled.

Her dark moods never lasted long. She always forgave
me quickly, and in that way seemed mercurial. I knew
that she was a Gemini, the twins, and I saw that change-
ability as evidence of her zodiac sign. She could show one
face to me in anger and then another not long after. I
used to think that's what it meant, the little gold symbol
she kept attached to her keychain. Both my parents had
one; whereas my father kept a tiny gold glove hanging
from his, a memento of the Golden Gloves boxing cham-
pionship he'd fought in, she'd attached to hers a small
charm of the Janus mask, the dual faces of tragedy and
comedy. She'd gotten it in college to commemorate her

membership in the drama troupe, but it might as well have been a symbol of her nature. Over the years it was the mask of Thalia—the laughing face—that she wore most often: her true face, like her thoughts, remaining mostly hidden from me.

I WANTED NOTHING MORE THAN TO PLEASE MY mother. At school I had begun to excel not only in reading and writing but also in math, a development that seemed to surprise and delight her. To reward me she brought home a doll I had been asking for and placed it at the top of the stairs. It sat there while I worked to complete the equations in my math homework. As my mother read aloud the questions and awaited my answers, I could see it, still in its cellophane wrapping, just over her shoulder. I don't know how long I delayed answering. Breaking my reverie, she spoke sharply: "You will not have that doll until you've gotten every equation right."

Had I been daydreaming about playing with it, casting my eyes furtively toward the landing? Or had I tilted my head up in that direction deep in thought, as if to pull the answer from the ether? It was clear to me then: the thing I had desired was reward for perfection, attainable if I were smart enough, and that my mother's happiness would depend on my performance. I was overcome with shame. Even now something of it comes back to wound me. What is it: That I wore my desire so plainly on my face, or that I was misunderstood—that we were as unknowable to each other then as now?

As the days grew shorter I spent all my time after dinner in my playroom—close enough to hear my mother turn the pages of her book in the kitchen. Sitting at my own small table, I mirrored her at hers, reading or mothering the doll she'd bought me—the way she cradled her chin in her hand, looking up from her work in thought, or the set of her jaw as when she scolded me. There was a smooth pattern to our days, a time in which my play with the doll looked exactly as our lives did then: no one to interrupt our togetherness, to intrude upon the story of mother and daughter.

My mother could not have known the imprint our few months alone together in a new place would make on me or how fiercely I would cling to the two-ness of us, the dyad of mother and daughter. Nor that my sense of filial duty, heightened now that we were far from home, could engender in me not only my obedience but also my silence. When I try to imagine what my mother was thinking that year, a young woman of twenty-eight years on the cusp of her new life, I find few clues in the letters she wrote to my father. "Things are going well," she told him. "I've gotten a job in Underground Atlanta at a restaurant called the Mine Shaft."

HOW LONG AFTER THAT LETTER WAS IT, THE EVEning my mother called me out of my playroom to meet a man standing in our kitchen doorway? He was tall and slim, his face outlined by long sideburns. He looked at me a little sideways, one of his eyes seemingly larger than the other, open wider.

"Joel, this is Tasha," my mother said to him. I could see that his hand trembled a bit as he moved farther into the kitchen and reached for the back of a chair.

"What should I call you?" I asked.

Something about the way he answered unsettled me, and I wondered if my mother noticed it too. "You can call me whatever you like," he said, grinning, his smile uneven, a twitch in his upper lip when he fixed his mouth to say *you*.

I shook my long braids, as was my habit, as if to banish a thought. "I'll call you Big Joe," I said, skipping out of the kitchen and back to my playroom. He was Big Joe to me from then on, the name sealing a kind of relationship between us that later would remind us both that he was not my father.

Perhaps that's what made me wary of him—something in his gestures—even as he played the role of helpful boy-friend to my mother, volunteering to babysit me in the afternoons whenever she was in class. I began to see him regularly. On the days that he kept me we'd often take drives around the city, a pattern that came to define many of our interactions over the years. He seemed to like driv-ing without a particular destination, as if simply to be in the car he spent so much time attending to—a black Ford Galaxie with a spotless white interior, whitewall tires, and chrome accents he'd polish till they shone.

I'd sit far against the passenger door, trying to breathe in fresh air from the barely open window as he smoked, the glowing embers at the tip of his cigarette like a flash-ing red light when he inhaled. I was careful not to fidget, or do anything to attract his attention, speaking only if he addressed me. The bass notes from the music on the eight-track stereo thumped like my own heartbeat grown louder—Curtis Mayfield singing "Freddie's Dead" or "Pusherman." What I could understand in those songs made me both sad and anxious, as if the album were not the soundtrack to a movie but to the story of my time with Big Joe, some part of my new life in Atlanta. When the track changed and "Superfly" came on, he sang along, his voice a shaky falsetto, just off-key. Outside the window, the landscape, like the music, repeated. I didn't know it then, but we were driving 285, the bypass loop around Atlanta.

Those drives were always lessons; the earliest one I recall was how to tell when you were being followed by a police officer in an unmarked car. "There'll be a hump like a little head in the center of the dashboard," he told me, as if it were something I would need to know. From then on, I watched to see how often he glanced at the rearview mirror, and I checked too, hoping someone might indeed be there behind us.

Each time we arrived back at the apartment I let out a sigh of relief. No matter how many times I rode with him, I never stopped worrying that he would abandon me somewhere and that I would lose my mother forever. I chastised myself for thinking such terrible things and banished them again and again. It's a kind of magical thinking, the way children come to believe they can cause certain events, the way the obsessive-compulsive believes certain talismanic acts must be performed to prevent disaster—that disaster can somehow be prevented. The lessons of mythology do not bear this out; had anyone believed Cassandra, so much could have been prevented. Yet no one did.

There is another way of looking at the myth of Cassandra's burden. Since no one believes her admonitions anyway, perhaps she begins to think that only her silence can prevent what is to come. Better to keep some things to herself rather than speak of them and invite disaster with her words.

I did not tell my mother anything about those afternoons with Big Joe, nor that I was afraid of what, one day, he might do.

WHEN I THINK BACK TO THAT LONG-AGO NIGHT, watching my mother dress for her job at the Mine Shaft in Underground Atlanta, I cannot recall whether she knows him yet, the man who will become my stepfather. Perhaps it is the night they meet. I know only that it is winter, and already the daffodils are blooming in Atlanta. I know that I have picked them for her, a handful of yellow narcissi—the flowers planted, in the myth of mother and daughter, to lure Persephone to her doom: kidnapping by the lord of the underworld. She picks a bright flower and the earth splits open beneath her, taking her into its dark throat.

It's as though I had rewritten the myth, passed the doom onto my mother as easily as I had handed her that rough bouquet of daffodils. That night, descending to work beneath the city, my mother was already entering an underworld from which she would never fully emerge.

[ ]

When I begin to say out loud that I am going to write about
my mother, to tell the story of those years I've tried to forget,
I have more dreams about her in a span of weeks than in all
the years she's been gone. She comes back to me, first, in the
house of my early childhood, my grandmother's house. I am
a child again in it, watching her go about domestic tasks:
hanging wet sheets on the line, ironing, or leaning into her
sewing machine, a few pins held between her lips. In other
dreams she appears in scenes from my current life, in places
she's never been, unrecognizable at first, as though she were
someone I'd not yet met. I am startled to see her then, and
always I am older than she is, older than she ever was. When
I dream us back into the house we shared with Joel, he is
there too. But I am not a child, and I know I have lived the
last thirty years without her. I know, too, that he has been
released from prison after all this time, but somehow he has
not killed her yet. I am aware, in the dream, that this makes
no sense and yet I still believe it, so I struggle to think of
ways to keep her alive. In the last dream I have, she is the old
woman she never became, thin and slightly stooped, her hair
silvery gray. We are in a room I've never seen, and I watch as
she walks around it, moving slowly, touching several objects
on shelves, on a table. It's as if, at the end of a long life, she is

contemplating the things she's collected over the years. When I wake, I try desperately to recall them, certain that those objects hold the story of who she was, the parts thus far unknowable to me. Then it hits me: I've not actually seen the objects she touched. The whole time, her back was to me.

3.

SOUL TRAIN

A PHOTOGRAPH FROM MAY 1974 MAKES PLAIN A certain truth: it is no longer just the two of us and, already, I am beginning to distance myself, to inhabit the periphery of my mother's new life. In every family, at some point, there must be someone who feels like an outsider: the one always standing or sitting a little farther from the group in pictures; the older sibling when a new baby comes along; the child from a previous marriage, sometimes with a different last name. Suddenly, I was all of those.

"I have a surprise for you," my mother said. It was late August 1973, months before the photograph would record into evidence the subtle but seismic shift set in motion by her announcement. I'd spent all of summer vacation at my grandmother's house in Mississippi and now my mother had come to take me back to Atlanta. It had been three months since I'd seen her.

"You have a new baby brother," she said, as declarative and matter-of-fact as she'd always been. "And Joel and I are married. We've moved to a new apartment where you have a much larger room down the hall."

Just before that, before I knew that everything had changed, she had seemed the same to me as when I'd left her in early June. I'd not noticed any change in her body then, no indication that she had begun to carry this new person I would meet. Had I even known where babies came from? I was seven years old. All summer I'd watched *The Brady Bunch*. In that moment, standing speechless before my mother, I turned the premise of the show over in my head, trying to make sense of this disruption. I asked no questions, though, deciding then that Big Joe must have come to the marriage with a baby just as my mother had come with me. The Brady family narrative had prepared me, providing a recognizable pattern of events and lending form to the chaos I felt. *You now have a stepfather and a stepbrother*, I told myself. Even now I do not know if my mother knew this was the story I held on to for years, telling it again and again to distance myself from this new family I did not want.

In the photograph, Joey is nine months old. He is holding himself up, both hands on the edge of the coffee table, my mother and Big Joe sitting just behind him on the sofa. In the tight frame of their proximity they form a triptych that reads "family." I am on the far end of the sofa. The only thing that seems to connect me is that I am sitting exactly as my mother is, a smaller version of her gestures written in my body's language.

What you can't see in the picture are Joel's feet. Beneath the coffee table, they seem now to represent everything to come that was troubling and distorted in our household, all of it hidden from view. I knew so little about him, and anything that seemed odd to me he would explain by mentioning the war. *Vietnam*, he would say. When he refused to eat spaghetti, it was because of the "worms" he'd seen while in the army; *Vietnam*, when I asked about his feet. On both of them, in strange symmetry, the second and third toes seemed to have been cut off at the first joint, the soles dry and deeply lined. Each toe was capped by a small, misshapen sliver of nail. *Vietnam*, he said when he saw me staring at them. Most likely he'd been born that way, the toes not fully formed. Perhaps he was ashamed to admit that, inventing a story connected to the war instead. I think now there was something wounded and vulnerable in the appearance of his feet, though as a child I felt only a mix of fear and revulsion when I looked at them. Before he and my mother were married I'd known only his slightly bulging eye, the way his hands trembled and his lips quivered around a cigarette; now I saw each day his strange, unsettling feet, the truncated digits.

Sometimes, when I went down to the kitchen for a glass of water late at night, he'd be sitting in dim light, drinking and singing quietly along with the record into a microphone attached to the stereo. That same shaky falsetto I'd come to know, but strained, as if he were struggling to prove he had somewhere inside him the soul of an artist. There were signs of his attempts everywhere: how he tried again and again to draw. First it was the figure in a newspaper ad for a learn-by-mail art school: *Can you draw me? If so, you can be an artist.* To which he contributed the skewed outline of a cartoon deer in profile. Then later, the Atlanta Falcons symbol he drew in silver oil paint for the wheel cover on the back of his van. For years, when I watched him drive away, I'd see the wheel cover, its black negative space surrounding a misshapen bird that may as well have been the symbol of his soul.

THE NEW APARTMENT WAS AT LEAST IN THE SAME school district, and I was relieved not to have to leave Venetian Hills. There were several young families with

kids near my age in the complex, too, so it wasn't hard to
make friends. The first family we met, the Dunns, had
five boys only a few years apart. I loved how loud and
boisterous they were, how they could dance and sing like
the Jackson Five and were always laughing and teasing
each other—*joning*, they called it. In Mississippi, when
we'd played the dozens we had called it *janking*. Because
I could come back with a good jone every now and then,
the boys took me in and treated me like a little sister.
After school we'd practice that ongoing dialectic with
the other children in the complex, each of us determined
to prove our ability to think fast, to be clever. It wounds
me now to think of it: *Your mama so fat . . .* , we said;
your mama so poor . . . ; *so cheap . . .* ; *your mama voice so
deep . . .* Sometimes the game got out of hand and someone would take offense, then revert to name calling and
pointing. That's when we'd shut it down: "Don't point
at me," we said, "my mama ain't dead." None of us ever
imagining it could be otherwise.

When we weren't involved in those displays of verbal
dexterity, we listened to 45s on my small record player or
jumped on pogo sticks to see who could stay on the lon-
gest. Our apartment and the Dunns' faced each other,
both end units in a cul-de-sac bordered by a small grassy
area where we played dodge ball and, beyond it, a tangle

of woods. The redbrick two-story buildings were unremarkable except for the large drainage system that ran
right through the complex—concrete culverts six feet
tall and flooded with light. Sometimes we'd lead expedi-
tions there, a group of us pretending the drain was a cave
and the small stream of water flowing through it a river
leading us out toward the sea. We were free to roam, and
nowhere we went in the complex was so far away that
we couldn't hear our mothers' voices calling us back for
dinner.

ONE EVENING I CAME HOME TO SOMETHING UNEX-
pected: the largest pot of water I'd ever seen boiling on
the stove and several live lobsters in the sink. My mother
seemed almost giddy as she prepared for our celebration,
gliding around the kitchen as Al Green's "I'm Still in
Love with You" played on the stereo. She'd completed all
her coursework to graduate with a master's in social work,
but we were celebrating Joel, too. He had been working
as a maintenance man at a residential facility for former
juvenile offenders, but that day—perhaps to impress my
mother or live up to some promise he'd made—he had
just enrolled in technical school.

In a photograph taken that night they look like performers in a 1970s soul band, bell-bottoms and Afros, both of them posed with one hand on the stair railing and one foot trailing behind on the step as if they are walking in unison down the stairs. Both dressed in white, like Al Green on the album cover propped up against the wall: my mother in a white jumpsuit and Joel in a white knit shirt and slacks. If there was one night, out of all those years, that my mother looked truly happy, that would have been it.

What I remember most from that night was the party. After dinner we went across the street to the Dunns' apartment. There were several families there, and as the kids raced around the apartment, the adults danced and drank from paper cups. Whenever a song came on we liked, the children all danced, too, crowding the floor to do the Bump, the Four Corners or the Loose Booty—a dance that involved rotating in a circle and twirling an arm above your head as if swinging a lasso. When the Jackson Five's "Dancing Machine" came on, my mother was in the center of the room, the colored lights from the homemade disco ball swirling around her as she smiled and launched into the Four Corners, rotating her hips in a semicircle, alternating single and double time. She was even more beautiful when she was dancing, and for a moment everyone seemed to gravitate toward her. The crowd split then, two rows forming on either side of her as she made her way down the middle of the Soul Train line.

I WOULD THINK OF THIS MOMENT, ONLY NINE years later, when the gathering of mourners in front of the church house cleaved to allow the pallbearers to carry her casket to the hearse.

4.

LOOP

OFTEN I WONDER WHETHER THE COURSE OF OUR lives would have been different had I told my mother, early on, the things she could not have known: the ways Joel had begun to torment me when she was not at home. Would she have wanted to save me right then? And in so doing, gotten out of the marriage early enough to save herself? Why didn't I tell? When I try to make sense of it now, I can't understand why I did not confide in her, and I can't help asking myself whether her death was the price of my inexplicable silence. I remember believing that I was a good child, that I was good because I did not complain, that I could suffer through my own trials and protect my mother from the difficult knowledge of how her life with a new husband was affecting me.

I don't recall exactly when it began, punishment as the pattern of my interactions with Big Joe whenever we

were alone. Always, there was some small thing he'd ac-
cuse me of, some transgression he invented in order to
punish me. "I know how to fix you," he'd say. "You're
like those retarded kids where your mother works and
you need to be committed." He'd tell me to pack my
bags, and stand over me in my room as I emptied the
contents of my chest of drawers into a suitcase. Then he'd
load me into the car as I sobbed.

You can drive Interstate 285, the bypass loop around
metro Atlanta, for a long time, depending on traffic, before making a full revolution. Joel would drive me around
for nearly an hour, saying nothing, until he decided I'd
had enough. Then he'd take me back home, my face
streaked and puffy, hours still before my mother would
return. Though he did this again and again, the threat
he made always the same, I was young enough, or frightened enough, to believe that he would one day carry out
his promise, that no amount of pleading or suffering would
make him turn the car around.

It occurs to me only now that my childhood obsessions must have had something to do with this. If you
had asked me then for my three biggest fears, I would
have listed being wrongly imprisoned when innocent,
committed when mentally sound, and buried still alive.
Each of these has something to do with powerlessness, of
being at the mercy of forces beyond your control. I had

read somewhere that the Victorians, as a precaution, tied a string around the finger of a person being buried and attached it to a little bell above the grave. The possibility of being laid out in a morgue, mistaken for dead, terrified me. I can see now that it was about being unable to move or cry out for help.

By the time I was in the fourth grade I had begun to have frequent dreams in which I could sense someone in the room, perhaps talking over me, but I could neither cry out nor move my limbs. I remember struggling even to move my little finger, knowing that I needed to wake myself up. Researchers call this state, when one is in between sleep cycles, *sleep paralysis*. Your mind begins to wake up but your body is still in a relaxed state, and so you cannot move for several minutes. You are conscious but have no control, the mind and body temporarily divided. Perhaps this division is a metaphor for the way I've lived all these years: the conscious mind struggling to move on, but the body resistant. The mind forgetting, the body retaining the memory of trauma in its cells.

If trauma fragments the self, then what does it mean to have dominion over the self? You can try to forget. You can go a long time without making a full revolution, but memory is a loop. When I moved back to Atlanta, a decade and a half after my mother's death, I would go miles out of my way to avoid driving 285. I thought that was enough, that if I didn't drive that loop, the worst memories would be kept reliably at bay. The truth, however, was waiting for me in my body and on the map I consulted to navigate my way around: how the outline of 285 bears the shape of an anatomical heart imprinted on the landscape, a wound where Memorial intersects it.

5.

PARDON

MY MOTHER IS SITTING ON THE BED, CHANGING Joey's diaper. I have come into the room and am standing in front of the door that opens into the bathroom, the large mirror behind the vanity catching not only my profile, but also the television across the room. All week long it has been tuned to the same channel, the same program. I have seen President Nixon's face again and again, and I know vaguely what is going on: there is trouble because the person occupying our nation's house has betrayed us. And now the new president is on the screen. I am stuck in place, watching, when Big Joe walks into the room. For a moment we are all together, the culmination of our domestic dilemma—"an American tragedy"—playing out on-screen. I can see, almost simultaneously, my reflection in the mirror, my mother folding the used diaper so that only the unsoiled exterior is visible, and Gerald Ford's face as he speaks: "It could go on and on and on, or someone must write the end to it."

6.

YOU KNOW

YOU REMEMBER EVEN THOUGH YOU DON'T WANT to: your mother saying, *Big Joe wants to adopt you*; saying, *He wants you to have his last name.* She is wearing a wan smile, one you see on your own face sometimes—the corner of her bottom lip pulling away as if not to participate in the act of smiling. There is something in her voice at once vaguely supplicant and matter-of-fact. You are in the fifth grade and this is the first time you hear it. When she tells you, you think, *Oh, because we are like the Brady Bunch*, and, in the *Brady Bunch* version of a blended family, no one has a different last name. It is 1976 and you have moved to the suburbs, into a four-bedroom house: a Tudor-style split-level with a tan and brown exterior that reminds you of the Brady home. Even at your age you know this is some version of the American dream: a house in the suburbs, and inside it a happy family—each member linked by the same last name.

The name of your subdivision is on a big sign at the entrance. Something pretentious like Canterbury—though you can't now remember exactly—the curved brick and bold script meant to impart an air of idyllic community. In a development of nearly identical houses, each one a slight variation of the others, yours is the one that draws the neighborhood children to play, the one with an aboveground swimming pool surrounded by a built-in deck. You spend the whole summer out there, and when not in the pool you are out exploring. There is a narrow strip of woods behind the house and a creek that separates the backyard from the three-hole golf course just beyond it. You collect shiny stones from the creek bed, follow carpets of moss growing on the north sides of trees, pretending escape like Harriet Tubman and the runaway slaves you've read about. You drop stones behind you to mark the path back, as in a fairy tale. The scent of muscadines in their thick skins draws you into the tangle of vines, where you pluck handfuls. This is a place for someone like you to spend as much time as you can away from the house. You who like to seek as much as you like to hide, to be invisible yet still in earshot of your mother's voice.

————

THIS IS A YEAR OF BIG CHANGES. YOU HEAR YOUR mother on the phone saying, "Mama, I have a new job! I'll even get to travel"; hear her as well in that other voice she uses on the phone with strangers, "No, I do not wish to become pregnant at this time"; hear her telling Big Joe, "Yes, I will talk to her about it." You know you are the *her*. You know because you are always listening, even when the adults think you are not.

This is a year of big changes and now he wants you to change your last name. You tell your mother no. "I want to keep my last name," you say. You don't want a new name to erase your father's. More than that, you don't want Joel to erase the person you have been your whole life. "She wants to keep her name," you hear your mother say, her voice sounding tired as she says it.

————

HERE IS A PHRASE YOU OVERHEAR: *WHITE FLIGHT.* At first you don't know what it means. You think of your new friend Missy, her father a pilot, a pair of tiny wings affixed to his lapel. In the neighborhood there are still a few white families left, For Sale signs in each of their yards. You've made friends with the girls in two of those houses—the only girls near your age on the street: Tina and her sister Susan, and Missy, an only child like you used to be. They tell you they knew the white people who lived in your house before you, how they swam in your pool all the time. You like hanging out with them because they are a couple of years older and talk about things you haven't heard of. In Tina's room the four of you flip through a stack of magazines—*Tiger Beat* and *Teen Beat*—and Tina reads the articles out loud: "You Can Have More Sex Appeal! It's Not Hard!" and "The Right Way to Kiss a Bay City Roller." They swoon over the cover featuring Leif Garrett, a teen idol you've never seen. "Adidas," Tina says. "Know what it stands for? 'All Day I Dream About Sex.'" She is laughing, her teeth shining. You laugh, too. You want them to like you.

Maybe that's why you do it, show them the magazines you've discovered at your house, on the floor of the closet beneath Joel's clothes—a stack nearly three feet tall: *Penthouse* and *Hustler* and *Swank*. You want them only to see that you know about these things, but Tina makes you sit down on the floor and pull out the magazines one by one so the four of you can flip through the pages. She points to the captions beneath the cartoons and tells you to read them aloud. When you stop at a word you don't want to say she nudges your shoulder:

"Go ahead." Her voice is older now, much older than you are. You wish you'd never brought them here, and you feel the emotion that stays with you the most, shame. Like you, the characters in the cartoons are black.

Tina is smiling broadly now, as if already beginning to laugh at the next cartoon on a page you haven't yet reached. "Do you know what MARTA stands for?" she says. You answer quickly, relieved to not be reading the captions and excited because you know this. You have ridden MARTA. "Of course," you say, rolling your eyes. "It stands for Metropolitan Atlanta Rapid Transit Authority." Tina shakes her blond head. "Nope," she says, leaning toward you. "It means 'Moving Africans Rapidly Through Atlanta.'" Missy and Susan are laughing before she even finishes the whole thing. You offer a wan smile, imagining their invisible wings: the three of them poised to fly away instead of riding the bus.

Once school starts you never see Tina and Susan again, but Missy offers to walk with you, since you are new. That first morning she knocks on the door and Joel comes into your room to tell you a white girl is waiting for you downstairs. "What her daddy do?" he says. But you misunderstand him; you make the mistake of thinking he is asking about *your* father. You beam with pride when you say it: "My father is a writer and a professor." "Not *your* daddy, *hers*," Joel says. "I don't care what your daddy do."

———————

THIS IS THE YEAR THAT JOEL HAS FINISHED TECH-
nical school, and now he has his own business: refrigera-
tion, air-conditioning, and heating repair. Working odd
hours, he is often home when your mother is not, his custom van or his Monte Carlo with the white ragtop parked
in the driveway just below your bedroom window. Before
you leave your room, to know if he is in the house, you
have learned to look for his vehicle in the driveway, just as
you know to listen for the sound of the garage door opening, a sign that your mother is finally home from work.

You can't wait to hear your mother's voice when you
get home from school. Afternoons are different now
that she has a new job. She leaves for work earlier and
gets home later, two hours later than you do. Now the
first thing you do when you come in the house is shut
off the alarm and call her office. Her business card is
taped to the wall beside the phone: GWENDOLYN GRIM-
METTE, PERSONNEL DIRECTOR, GEORGIA RETARDATION
CENTER. The friendly secretary you've never met sounds
delighted each time she hears your voice. "Hello there,"
she says, "won't your mother be pleased to hear you've
called!" You ask her how her day is going. You are a polite
child and you want to make your mother proud. You do
your homework without being told; you keep your room

perfectly neat, everything in its place. You are happiest when adults are pleased with you, your mother most of all.

Which is why it troubles you when she confronts you about your hair. "Big Joe told me your ponytail hasn't been looking too good when you leave for school," she says. You are a big girl now; you've been doing your own hair in the mornings for a year and this makes it seem like you are regressing, like you cannot be trusted to properly attend to your appearance. Like you would go out of the house looking unkempt, an embarrassment. She is not there to see you walk out the door, so his story is *the* story. Just like last year, when you were still in the apartment, and he told her you had been sleepwalking. That he'd found you in the middle of the night downstairs, knocking on the neighbors' door, and had to guide you back upstairs, back to bed.

Now she wants to know what is going on with your hair. You do not tell her about your hairbrush. You are meticulous, everything in your bathroom neatly arranged and in its proper place: your hairbrush, clean of hair or grease, in the top drawer of the vanity. You don't tell her that lately you've been finding it out on the counter in the afternoons when you get home from school or, worse, in the drawer when you reach for it in the morning, full of hair: his hair, greasy from the oil he uses to treat his scalp, flakes of dandruff clinging to the bristles. Even now you don't know why you never said anything.

———————

ONE DAY YOU ARE SICK AT HOME IN BED WITH A fever so high you are delirious. You dream you are prone in a white room: white walls, white ceiling, everything white, so much white that you cannot see where the ceiling ends and the walls begin. A white box. Though you are not aware of your body, your mind is alert, watching, which is how you know you are lying down. Because you are looking up at the ceiling, a canopy of white, when it happens: an opening like a trapdoor out of which filth comes raining down and covers you.

———————

YOU ARE IN MRS. MATHIS'S FIFTH-GRADE CLASS-room at Clifton Elementary. This is the fourth time in five years that you have moved, the third time you've had to change schools. Lucky for you, you love this school as much as the last two, particularly because of Mrs. Mathis. You love her serious, no-nonsense demeanor, the way her gray-brown hair frames her face like a cap, how when she does not believe something she's told, she says, "That's a bunch of bull," peering over the top of her glasses, her hands balled into fists on her hips. You listen with fascination to her stories—most of them about growing up in Southern Rhodesia, the daughter of white missionaries, what it was like being a white person in a black country. Perhaps it was not so different from this: because now she is a white teacher in a mostly black school. When you listen to her you think about your grandmother in Mississippi, how she would refer to some folks as "good white people," and you know Mrs. Mathis must be one of them. Where you come from, good white people are not hard to recognize.

This is the year you discover Ulysses S. Grant. In the library at school you have found a biography of him and fallen in love with this leader of the Union Army, a good white man opposed to slavery, a champion of civil rights for black people. You check the book out and carry it around for days, looking at the picture of him on the cover, his bearded face reminding you of your father.

What you know of Abraham Lincoln makes you love him, too, and what you know of him specifically is the Emancipation Proclamation and the Gettysburg Address. *Fourscore and seven years ago our fathers brought forth, on this continent, a new nation, conceived in liberty, and dedicated to the proposition that all men are created equal. . . .* You memorize the whole thing. When you are bored or anxious, you recite this speech over and over in your head. At the Civil War graveyard between the school and home you often stop to read the stones, make grave rubbings. Over the graves of Confederate soldiers, you recite it out loud, your voice rising each time you say "all men are created equal."

AT THANKSGIVING YOUR GRANDMOTHER TRAVELS from Mississippi to see the new house, her face beaming with pride when she hangs the draperies she's made for each room. You watch her fill an entire album with Polaroid instant photographs of all the new furniture, every angle of the house's interior and exterior, even the name on the mailbox: GRIMMETTE.

This is the name that is not your name, the name that makes you different from everyone in your household. But it is not only your name that makes you different. You are special. For you, your grandmother has done her most elaborate work. The draperies in your room are gold and antique white brocade crowned by a cornice and swags with little tassels. The swags are like scalloped icing on a birthday cake. There is a matching bedspread, dust ruffle, and canopy. Days later, when she leaves for the airport, you shut your door behind you, lie in the center of the bed looking up at the canopy, your head on a bolster pillow trimmed in gold fringe. To stop crying, you pretend you are some kind of princess. You call yourself Leilani because you think, with your deep tan skin and long, dark hair, you look Hawaiian. Princess Leilani: your imagination carries you far from where you are.

At school you play a princess, too. You are the teacher's pet in Mrs. Mathis's class, so it is no surprise when you are chosen to act the lead—a princess in a play called *The Reluctant Dragon*. Rehearsals last for two weeks and you go to school each day happy to pretend you are someone else. At the parent-teacher meeting, Mrs. Mathis tells your mother that you are "always an eager student, devouring lessons and moving on to the next one before anyone else."

When you finish assignments early, you read the entire collection of books Mrs. Mathis keeps on a shelf in the corner: the Hardy Boys, Nancy Drew, Encyclopedia Brown. You write a novella about a girl your age, far away in the English countryside, who solves a mystery involving a weather vane: "The Mystery of the Misdirected Weather Vane," after Nancy Drew's #33, *The Witch Tree Symbol*. Informing the plot is a phrase you learned from your grandmother: "When the sun is shining and it's raining, the devil is beating his wife." The key to the mystery lies in that seeming contradiction: that the sun could be shining during a thundershower, just as the weather vane could be made to point in the wrong direction.

Mrs. Mathis wants to take you to a countywide meeting of teachers, and your mother is delighted. She takes the yellow legal pad on which you've drafted the novella to work with her and the friendly secretary types your handwritten pages. Nowhere, in all sixty pages, is there mention of the main character's family or home life. At the teachers' meeting they marvel at your imagination, the story you've written about a place and an experience so different from your own.

———

THIS IS A YEAR OF BIG CHANGES. JIMMY CARTER has been elected president and your mother is invited to the inaugural ball. You know what a ball is because of Cinderella and you imagine your mother going to a place like that, wearing a fancy gown that your grandmother will make, until you hear your mother on the phone: "No, Mama, I'm not going to go. Joel wouldn't feel comfortable there, among those people." Even you know what this means.

———————

YOU ARE IN HEALTH CLASS FOR FIFTH GRADERS when you hear Bill Withers's "Lean on Me" as the soundtrack to a scene in a film about drug addiction. A policewoman has come to the classroom to talk about the dangers of illicit drugs and you sit in the semidark watching the screen as the reel sputters into action. When the song comes on there is a woman at the top of a stairwell. "This is what withdrawal from heroin looks like," intones the voiceover. The woman wears bell-bottom jeans and an Afro like your mother's and she is careening down the stairs, bouncing from one wall to the other, a substance white as milk spewing from her gaping mouth. Bill Withers is crooning his song, offering to be a friend when you need help carrying on, and you can't take it anymore. You have to leave the room. But you cannot forget what you saw. From now on each time you hear the song you will think of a woman who looks like your mother, in distress.

———————

YOU ARE IN THE FIFTH GRADE THE FIRST TIME YOU hear your mother being beaten. You have lived in the house only a few months, and sometimes your brother is still afraid to sleep in his new bedroom alone. His room is down the hall from yours, right next to the bedroom your mother and Joel share. There is only a thin wall between them. You tuck Joey into the top bunk and listen from the lower as he falls asleep. This is when you hear it, the loud smack as Joel's fist hits her. And then your mother's voice, almost a whimper but calm, rational: *Please Joel. Please don't hit me again.* For all you know this is the first time. Most likely it is not.

YOU ARE IN THE HALLWAY, JUST OUTSIDE YOUR fifth-grade classroom. Mrs. Mathis wants to know why you've left the classroom, why you won't watch the police film you are all required to see. She follows you into the girls' bathroom down the hall, wants to know what is going on, why you haven't been concentrating all day in class. She is standing with her fists on her hips, peering over the top of her glasses, when you say it:

"Last night I heard my stepfather hit my mother."

She is looking at you hard, her fists relaxing. Then her hands are on your shoulders and you hear it, the one phrase that tells you all you can expect: "You know," she says, "sometimes adults get angry with each other." When she turns you toward the door to go back to the classroom, you know there is nothing she is going to do.

YOU ARE IN THE FIFTH GRADE AND YOU ARE TIRED. You have barely slept the whole night. You can barely pay attention in school. All day you have thought about what to do. All day you have felt overwhelming shame each time you replay the sound of your mother's pleading voice. You decide that you must do something, regardless of what your teacher has told you. You think somehow you can protect her.

At home you catch your mother alone, sitting on the bed, her left temple dark and swollen. Standing in front of her, eye level, you shift your weight from one leg to the other, your head down. "Mommy," you say quietly, so as not to be overheard. "Do you know how, when you love someone and you know they are hurting, it hurts you, too?" You have waited until the whole sentence is out before looking up at her, directly in her eyes, doing everything you can to hold her gaze for the moment it takes until her mouth falls open. It's as if she is about to speak, but then she only nods, her lips pressed tight against any words.

Later that night you hear it, your mother's voice as she tells Joel, "Tasha knows."

You are ashamed and you don't know why. The need in the voice of your powerful, lovely mother is teaching you something about the world of men and women, of dominance and submission. You hear it emanate from the most intimate of spaces, the bedroom with its marriage bed. Your shame and your sadness are doubled. You hear in your mother's words a plea to get him to stop. You hear her desperate hope that his knowing *you* know, knowing *you* listen, will put an end to the abuse. As if the fact that you are a child, that you are only in the fifth grade, will change anything at all. And now you know that there is nothing you can do.

YOU KNOW YOU KNOW YOU KNOW.

LOOK AT YOU. EVEN NOW YOU THINK YOU CAN write yourself away from that girl you were, distance yourself in the second person, as if you weren't the one to whom any of this happened.

7.

DEAR DIARY

TO BE BESIDE ONESELF, IN THE IDIOM, IS TO BE SO
overcome with intense emotion, like grief or fear, as to
feel outside one's own body. Cognitive theorists suggest
that speaking about trauma or writing about it may help
heal the fissure in the fabric of selfhood brought on by
the event. I think now that's why my mother gave me
the diary. She knew that I was hurting, that her situation
had upset me; I had told her so.

In the aftermath of my *knowing*, the silence between
us widened. Joel's presence, his watchful eye, made it
harder for us to interact as mother and daughter, and she
and I were almost never alone. When Joel was around,
I retreated to my room, where I turned the volume up
on my record player, transforming the moves I learned
in ballet and gymnastics classes into the language of in-
terpretive dance routines I would perform at school. I

danced again and again to Roberta Flack's "The Impossible Dream" and Otis Redding's "(Sittin' on) the Dock of the Bay." In Redding's song, it was his melancholy that spoke to me, and the moment he sings of leaving his home in Georgia I would imagine what it would be like to get away from where I was. It was as if, even then, I knew that getting away was something I would do alone, that it would mean being without my mother, the sadness of that.

"The Impossible Dream" became an anthem for me: lines about fighting an unbeatable foe, bearing unbearable sorrow, righting an unrightable wrong and reaching an unreachable star. I would lose myself in the music and these words, silent as my body's choreography articulated what I could not speak: the need to right an unrightable wrong to which I had become witness. I did not yet know what it would mean to bear the unbearable sorrow, though I was beginning to know the fight I'd have to wage, the foe.

The diary gave me a crucial outlet. My mother knew that whatever else there was in me needing articulation I would have to write it down. I have always loved the feel of books, the way they give a literal weight to words and make of them a sacred object I can hold. I'd made my own books as soon as I'd learned to write, tying sheets of construction paper together with ribbon to make a spine, then inscribing my name on the frontispiece in the most ceremonial script I could manage. For this diary, my first, my mother had chosen a lined leather volume with a gold border around the front cover, and a brass lock with a tiny key. Inside, she inscribed these words: "For my daughter, Natasha, on her 12th birthday. Love, Mom." Even the edges of each page were tipped in gold, as if to add a shimmering frame to whatever I might write. I was thrilled to have a book for my thoughts, for my eyes alone.

That feeling was short-lived. It wasn't long before I came home from school one day to find the lock on the diary broken. "Who said you could go to Washington?" Joel said, standing in the doorway to my bedroom. I had been excited about the school trip for months, and my father had promised half the cost so that I would be able to go. "Mom did," I said, the diary in my hand open to the page on which I'd written of my excitement.

"We'll see about that," he said, turning to walk back down the hall.

When the time came, I was indeed allowed to go, most likely because my mother had intervened, perhaps telling Joel that my father would be upset when he found out that I was being kept from going on an educational field trip. I don't think Joel ever mentioned the diary to my mother, that he had broken the lock and read it.

Neither did I. Knowing that what had happened was between us alone, I was determined to respond on my own.

No longer was I content to describe my days, to begin my entries "Dear Diary," to write as if to an intimate friend, a second self. Instead, I turned the page on any notion of privacy, certain that he would read whatever I wrote, and began again.

"You stupid motherfucker!" I wrote. "Do you think I don't know what you're doing? You wouldn't know I thought of you like this if you weren't reading my diary." Each entry thereafter was a litany of indictments, my accounting of all the things he had done. Not only had I stopped expecting that my words could be private, but also I had begun to think of them as a near-public act of communication, with a particular goal, and that there could be power in articulating what I needed to say. Even more, there was something powerful in *writing* it. In my first act of resistance, I had inadvertently made him my first audience. Everything I'd needed to articulate came out in those pages, raw and unfiltered, and I felt for the first time in this new voice I inhabited a profound sense of selfhood. I could push back by not holding inside what might otherwise have continued to divide and erode me.

This was long before I knew what Joel was actually capable of, which allowed me a certain fearlessness. I was sure that he would not tell my mother, because that would mean he'd have to reveal what he was doing: invading the private world of the diary she had given me. I was also sure that he would never say anything to me about it, that he would rather pretend he'd never seen the words I had for him. From then on, when he looked at me, I'd return his gaze, the afterimage of my words in the space between us.

I had begun to compose myself.

8.

ACCOUNTING

ONE DAY I COME HOME FROM SCHOOL GIDDY WITH news. It is early evening and the four of us take our seats at the kitchen table. Most days during the week I have practice after school and get home too late for these "family" dinners. Joel will already have left the house on those nights, so there are blessed stretches of days when I don't see him at all.

Tonight, though, I'm too excited to save my news for when I can tell my mother alone, so I blurt it out as soon as we sit down. Not only have I been promoted to editor on the newspaper staff, but also, because of a short story I wrote, I've been invited to join Quill and Scroll, the club responsible for putting out the school literary journal. I can see the delight in my mother's face. She is smiling at me and I am like a daffodil, lifting my face to the sun. I go on about how much I love the short story reader we are using in English class, how John Updike's "A&P" is my favorite so far, how I am planning to write a new story for an upcoming issue. "I'm going to be a writer!" I announce.

"You not gonna do any of that," Joel says, shrugging his shoulders. He doesn't even look up from his plate when he says it. My mother is seated to my right and I see her out of the corner of my eye, a deep furrow between her brows, her jaw clenched so tight she seems to speak with her mouth closed: "She. Will do. WHATEVER. She wants."

I am stunned, my head bent now toward my own plate, afraid to look at her or provoke him further by meeting his eyes across the table. For years she has held her tongue, encouraging me mostly in private so as to avoid his jealous anger. This moment is different, and I know the cost. *She's going to be beaten tonight for that*, I think, the tone—even inside my head—resigned, matter-of-fact.

The rest of dinner we eat in silence, Joel glowering, my mother in quiet defiance. I am stealing glances at her face, thinking of the bruises she'll wear tomorrow, all the hidden places on her body soft with pain, calculating the price she'll keep paying to save me.

I'VE REPLAYED THIS SCENE IN MY HEAD COUNT-
less times: *She. Will do. WHATEVER. She wants.* Even
now I hear in my mother's voice, her measured restraint,
the origins of my own.

[   ]

When I try to write about my mother, those lost years I do not want to remember, everything is scattered. I write on a yellow legal pad, carrying it around with me until the pages come loose, torn from the adhesive at the top. I write on scraps—envelopes, receipts—and I misplace them. I record audio notes in my phone, my voice husky and unfamiliar. I write upside down in my unlined journal, in the center of it, as if my heart has been turned on end. I gather what I can, handwritten pages, notebooks and journals I've filled, yellow and white notepads stacked on my desk. I try to write about fire, our arrival in Atlanta. One day, I go online to do research on conflagration, how a car engine might burst into flame. That night, I sleep a deep and dreamless sleep and, in the morning when I wake, my house burns.

II.

9.

CLAIRVOYANCE

JUST WEEKS BEFORE HER DEATH, MY MOTHER VIS-
ited a psychic for a reading. This is a detail I've never been
able to let go. Beyond the transcripts of her phone conversations with Joel and the notes for a speech she wrote
on a legal pad, it is one of the few clues I have about the
contours of her last days. To enter that world, I have asked
myself the same questions: *How was she going about her
day-to-day life? What had she been thinking?*

I tell myself that I might find an answer through a
kind of experiential research, that making my own visit
to a psychic may reveal something useful in my attempt
to reconstruct the events of May 1985. I want to know
what she experienced in that hour with a medium, what
she might have taken away from the encounter. Was she
a skeptic, as I am? An agnostic willing to be convinced
with evidence? What I do not admit to myself is that

there is an undercurrent of desperation in my decision, that my visit to a medium might be more than simply academic, just as her visit might have been more than the entertainment she assured me it was back then.

My friend Cynthia knows a medium and offers to make an appointment for us to visit his apartment. I am willing to pay the $150 "just for the experience," I say, but I decide I don't want him to know anything about me. I tell her it is because of my skepticism, that I suspect he would use the internet to gather information before our meeting, so we agree that she will arrange the appointment, saying only that she'd like to bring a friend. As an added precaution, we agree also to give him a fake name when we meet: Cassandra. When the psychic opens the door at the appointed time, Cynthia introduces me as "Cassie."

The first thing I notice is his accent. He's a Brit, and offers to make us tea. He's making some for himself, and I read his offer as a way for him to learn some things about me, an attempt to get me chatting before the session begins. So I say very little, discussing the weather— already hot for early May—and sit down at the other side of his desk. The apartment seems new and sparsely decorated. There is a large computer monitor on the desk and I note that it is turned off, the screen dark. Cynthia sits to his right and a little behind him so he cannot see her face. I angle my body toward him and do not look at her. When we begin, I set my cell phone between us to record the conversation.

I've seen the performance of mediums on television, and our session begins in much the same way: He asks if two months mean anything to me, January and August. Often that is the moment someone in the audience or the person for whom the reading is being done will say, "Yes, that was my mother's birth month," or "That's when my father died." It provides a bit of a clue, a path the psychic might follow to try to extract more information in order to convince his subject that contact is being made. It is the first signal that the dead have supposedly emerged with messages for the living. The living—wanting so much to believe—unwittingly provide all the necessary information for the medium to guess some aspects of their lives and thus weave a story they want desperately to hear. It's a beautiful con. But I am determined to be unreadable, or readable only for misdirection, and to give him as little as possible, or nothing at all. I am hiding the reason I have come.

January and August. These are the birth months of Joel and my brother, Joey. I think for a moment and decide to tell the medium this. "Yes, something's coming through," he says. "I don't know if they are still alive or not . . ." He pauses, his words trailing off. "They are," I say, adding nothing more. I watch him with a look of mild anticipation, as if to say, *And?* He has a yellow legal pad in front of him on which he begins jotting things down, dates and numbers, phrases that, he says, he is beginning to hear as the dead sidle up to him to speak. I think instead that he must realize he's already reached a dead end and is considering a new approach. I am reading the medium, too, using what must be a similar methodology. He is perhaps in his late fifties or early sixties, white. His curly hair, worn on the longer side, is gray.

For the next half hour he tries various avenues to get information, to get me talking. He begins by asking if someone in my family had traveled a lot, perhaps in the military. I am almost fifty years old, and Cynthia is closer to sixty, and white. Looking at me, and the two of us together, he can assume that there is a good chance I am of an age that I might have a parent who was in the service—most likely during the Vietnam War. I decide to tell him that my father was in the navy—but I do not tell him the Canadian navy—and that he died in 2014. I do it to give him something easy, a line to follow in order to see what he will come up with, guessing. I do it so as not to reveal anything of why I am really there.

My whole life people have wondered "what" I am, what race or nationality. It is familiar to me, the way the medium is trying to figure out my origins. It's happened again and again: someone looking at me furtively, or calling me "exotic" and asking "What's your heritage?" Once, when I was making a purchase in a department store, the white salesman behind the counter was too nervous or too polite to ask—most likely not wanting to offend a white woman by assuming that she was anything but white. He needed to write, on the back of my check, the additional identifying information required back then: race and gender. Hesitating, his pen hovering, he tried to look at me without my notice. I watched his face as he deliberated after a second and third glance at my features, my straight, fine hair, my skin color and clothing. He must have considered, too, how I had spoken and whether any of those factors matched his notions of certain people—black people. I stood there and said nothing as he scribbled the letters *WF*: the designation for white female. In the same week, with a different clerk, I had been given the designation *BF*. That time I had not been alone: I had been standing in line at the grocery store with a friend who is black. Now the medium is scribbling on his notepad, writing the letters *NA*. There are several ways the believer might seize upon that detail. In the moment, however, I am thinking only one designation of those letters, how he is writing them over and over: *Not Applicable. Not Applicable. Not Applicable.* As if nothing we are doing will bring me the answers I need.

It is necessary that I say something occasionally to keep the reading going, so I decide to tell him that, indeed, my father had sailed around the world—a reasonable assumption given his naval service—and the medium seems to be assuming that my father met my mother in one of those exotic places he traveled. Still, I can see that he cannot guess my racial origins. My reticence leaves him with only guesswork, and the details he gets wrong serve only to harden my skepticism. I must be smirking a bit when he says that not only am I "very clever," but I "hide [my] thought processes well."

Another tactic: now he is writing the word *May*.

"I keep getting something about May," he says, "a name, someone in your family?"

"No," I say, shaking my head.

"May, May. I don't know—just think about it," he says. It is not a name of someone in my family. It is the month of May and he is shrewdly surmising the month must hold some significance for me since it is the very month I have come to see him. And of course, it does.

"Something is coming through, but it's a little distant and I'm having a hard time hearing. Sometimes they don't step close enough, but your father has. He wants you to know how proud he is of you."

When he tells me this, I can't stop the emotion welling up in my eyes. In my rational mind I know this is nothing the medium has ascertained from speaking with my father, but it is true nonetheless—and I knew it long before he died. I am quietly weeping only because my father has been gone just a few months and my grief is still fresh.

It's the response he's been waiting for. This, the medium must deduce, is why I have come. There are common themes, archetypal themes, in families. This is the province of the medium: the dead want resolution, the medium assures us, or forgiveness, or peace. They want us to know they are OK and they want us to take care of ourselves, to find our own peace.

There is a range of images and general questions a medium can pose to make one believe he has established contact: *Is there someone who died too soon? I'm getting a fedora, the smell of a cigar.* These are things that most likely any of us would have some connection to—no matter how tenuous. He goes with "Has anyone lost a leg?" I decide to give him this information—let him run with it. Why not? I am waiting for my mother to speak. My grandmother lost a leg. My mother's mother.

NA NA, he writes. I could tell him these are the first two letters of my name—to which he might reply that he was getting that, that someone was telling him. Or I could tell him that these letters spell the name I called my grandmother: Nana.

The medium does not know whether or not my mother is dead and has said very little about her. He tells me my father is quite present, boisterous, doing all the talking. Even if my mother were there, he implies—not knowing whether she is living or dead—my father is sucking all the air out of the underworld, doing all the talking, and only my grandmother has managed to get a word in.

"May," he says again, tilting his head as he looks at me. The gesture is a prompt for me to finally realize what I have been missing all along, to say *Yes, of course!*—and still I don't. There is nothing left for him to do but wind down our session. "Your father is saying you need to take care of yourself," he tells me. "He's saying you'll want to come back and do this again; you'll *need* to."

When we leave I try to hide what I am thinking from Cynthia by talking only about how wrong the medium was, how hard he tried to figure out my race and why I was there. I don't tell her that for all my overt display of skepticism I would have given anything for a message from my mother, that I wanted more than anything for the medium's claims to make contact with the dead to be real.

Instead, I have only two options: to believe he was a fraud or to believe that, after all these years, my mother would not emerge to communicate with me: that she'd have nothing to say.

I WAIT UNTIL I FORGET MOST OF WHAT THE ME-
dium and I discussed before I listen to the recording of
our session. I wait, in fact, two years, carrying the record
of our conversation around with me on my phone under
the title "Medium" with the date below it and the time it
took: 5-6-2015; 1:22:46. When I walked out of his apartment, I knew that I wanted to experience it all over again,
for research, convinced that the distance would make
me even more dismissive of the whole enterprise. I'm
smug when I touch the Play button on the phone, smug
through nearly the entire session. Then I hear it, what
he'd been saying over and over two years earlier: *May,
May, May.* "Yes, it was May, the month before her death,
the fifth month of the year," I say out loud, watching as
the timer on my phone winds down the minutes. That's
when it hits me; he's a Brit and so if I write the date nu-
merically, as he might, in his calendar of appointments, it
would appear like this: day first, then month: 6-5-2015.
Americans would read that as June 5, which is the date
of the thirtieth anniversary of my mother's death. It hits
me so hard I weep.

Had I been so resistant that I didn't make room for
her to speak? Had she found another way to let me know
she was there?

Numerology is a kind of faith, a belief in the mysti-
cal relationship between numbers and events. Visiting
the medium, I had held out only the most remote hope
that my mother would speak through him, and even
barely admitted *that* to myself. I had never imagined that
I might find meaning in numbers instead. But now I
see that I've always been obsessed with numbers, both as
portents and as a way to make sense of my past—to see
the patterns they reveal, etched like constellations dis-
cernible only in the clearest night sky.

I have long held fast to the idea that my story is
written in my stars: that there was a pattern in place for
me beginning with my birth, a child of an interracial
marriage, on Confederate Memorial Day, exactly one
hundred years to the day, April 26, that it was first cel-
ebrated in Mississippi; pattern in that the only birthday
of my mother's I recall celebrating was her twenty-sixth,
when I decorated a cake in the shape of a halved water-
melon, twenty-six black seeds marking her time; in that
I marked my own twenty-sixth birthday with melancho-
lia, knowing it was the first time I'd reached an age I was
vividly aware that my mother had been; that the year
we moved to Atlanta, 1972, was the same year that the
Confederate monument on Stone Mountain was finally
completed; that my name means "resurrection" in Greek

and that I have had now what I think of as a second Jesus
year, counting down the thirty-three years it's been since
her death—my whole adult life without her. Before and
after. And now, that I have reached this second Jesus year
at age fifty-two, which of course is twenty-six doubled.

Irrational as it sounds, I have clung to the pattern
these numbers make so as to bring order to the chaos over
which I desperately need to believe I have control—or,
at least, that I have the power to recognize, just as the
ancients looked to the sky and saw the myths they lived
by writ large.

My rational mind knows very well what my irrational mind is doing. So why not let both exist simultaneously? This is, after all, how I make metaphor. And it is
how I find myself weeping with joy, suddenly, because I
have found a way to believe, at last, that this was a sign:
6-5-2015, the simple reversal of the numbers to reflect
the date as the British medium might have recorded it,
evidence that my mother was indeed present during my
session with him.

I am weeping with joy but the feeling is short-lived.
When my rational mind takes over again, I am left only
with a profound sense of absence: that, whether she had
been there or not, she still had no words for me. Soon, I
am weeping only at my own foolishness, my desperation.

10.

EVIDENCE

Last Words

THE MORNING OF MY MOTHER'S DEATH, THE PO-
lice entered into evidence a twelve-page document she'd
been writing, by hand, on a yellow legal pad. A note in
the top corner reads: "Taken from victim's briefcase
found in her bedroom. 6/5/85." It would be twenty-five
years before I ever saw these words.

I HAD HEARD ABOUT THE COUNCIL FOR BATTERED
Women a long time before I had any direct contact with
them. I read everything I saw and silently applauded their
work. I always felt that it was an agency I would like to
volunteer my services to when the kids grew up.

I always knew that I would get out of my marriage. It
was one of those things that never should have happened.

The reason it did was a combination of emotional black-mail and physical threats and intimidation. I never loved my husband and felt guilty about that, so I threw myself into being the best housewife/mother, employee around. He knew I didn't love him and always kept me off balance by falsely accusing me of running around on him. Relating back to an incident when we first met and I continued to see other people. His pet phrase was "I can't trust you." Since he always said he wasn't happy either, I assumed that we would bow out gracefully when our son left for college. On each of his birthdays, I counted off one more year. I got down to eight.

The beginning of the end started in the fall of 1978 when I changed jobs. Not to imply that there had not been trouble during the other nine years. I was thankful when it was a hole punched in the wall, or beaten into a cabinet with a hammer. My physical damage over the years ranged from black eyes, a hairline fracture of the jaw, to bruised kidneys, and a sprained arm, all for things he "thought" about. I quickly learned to gauge his moods and became a master at diffusing him. One of our problems was my successful employment. While he enjoyed the things my income allowed us to purchase, he was jealous of my success.

The new job came about as a surprise to me. I discussed thoroughly with him that my new duties would entail travel some overnights and occasionally long hours and we decided that I should take it.

The other major problem was my daughter from a previous marriage. He insisted that I loved her more than our son and while he was not overtly cruel to her he managed to do little things to keep her upset. If I attempted to intervene, it only made matters worse. She spent most of her pre-teen years in her room. At work I became a master at scheduling that would keep me out of town as little as possible. My co-workers soon learned not to invite me to happy hours or any activities after office hours because I always had an excuse. I had an excuse for myself, too—my children needed me, there would be time for activities later. While this wasn't 100% true, I knew I could never depend on my husband to "be there" when I needed him. Finally in the summer of 1983 I started doing things after ten years. Each time I did, my husband's reaction grew worse. His accusations and threats increased and for the first time, he had a gun. . . .

I REMEMBER THAT EVENING SO WELL. WE WERE *sitting at the kitchen table. He wasn't really angry, just talking matter-of-factly, but subtly threatening me at the same time. He remembered that a friend had given him a gun, and when he jumped up abruptly from the table and went outside, I was positive he was going to get it. I wanted to run, but the kids were asleep upstairs. So instead, I locked* the doors and called the police. When he returned I had just finished. He believed my explanation that I thought he was leaving and that was why I locked the door. When the police arrived, I dissolved into tears. He was all compassion, assuring the police that he would never hurt me, that he loved me very much and they left smiling. Afterwards he gave me a chilling look and said, "I don't like you calling the police on me," and picked up where he left off.

ONE OF HIS FAVORITE THINGS TO DO WAS TO HAVE "discussions" in the middle of the night. I've always needed eight hours of sleep, so he knew I would have a rough time at work. These discussions increased in frequency. I started having problems eating and sleeping. Finally at work one day I burst into tears and had to be taken away from my office—all behaviors heretofore foreign to me. My weight took a drastic drop and continued until size 3s were too big.

In August I went to visit my mom and to get my daughter from a summer visit. Needing to prepare her for my weight loss, I told her my husband had a drinking problem and we were having problems surrounding that. (I had never shared our problems with anyone.) As I left with my son, I told him I couldn't continue to live like that and that we needed counseling. I didn't expect a positive response because

I had tried the same thing five years ago and his response was "the only problem we have is that I can't trust you."

This time he fooled me and contacted a counseling service and made an appointment—meant for when I returned. While I was away I went to our family physician who diagnosed me as being depressed, and after my assurance that I was not suicidal, prescribed medication for me. His comment being "I can give you something to help you cope with the situation, but getting away from it is the only cure."

I enjoyed the counseling sessions. For the first time in 10 years I felt free to express all of the things that I had repressed for so long. One day the counselor told me that for the next week, to do whatever I felt like doing, and only that. I remember speeding down the expressway at dusk with the wind blowing my hair as being the most enjoyable thing I did.

What eventually happened after two months of therapy is that I realized that I didn't want to wait eight more years to get out of that relationship. I wanted out immediately. When I said that in one of our sessions, I could see the fury boiling in his eyes. It erupted with a string of profanity and he slammed out of the counselor's office. I sat there stunned. Not only at his reaction, but at the fact that I had the courage to say that in the first place. I wondered how I would get home because I didn't have bus fare, but when I looked outside he was waiting. He drove like a madman almost

*hitting a jogger and swearing out the window at him. I
huddled in my corner afraid to say anything.*

    *He went out immediately after we got home, and I was
both happy and apprehensive. I had a right to be apprehensive.
When he returned, he woke me and we went to the
kitchen for a "discussion." He sat at the table playing with
a knife. He had frequently threatened me with knives too.
(Once he drew a picture of how he was going to cut my face)
and told me quite calmly that since I had decided to leave
him he would kill me. He reminded me that he had said
he would if I left. I started pleading with him, and mentioned
the kids. His response was he would kill them too,
then himself . . .*

    *He told me he would be nice and let me choose the way
I wanted to die. When I didn't respond he put the knife
to my throat and said fine, he would kill me with it. So
I responded that I would take my prescription for my depression.
(I had most of the pills left because he didn't like
me taking them. One pill made me so groggy the following
day that I walked around in a daze.) With the knife at my
throat, I swallowed three pills before I passed out. The last
thing I remember is being half dragged and half carried
upstairs, placed on the bed. [Note in the margin: "several
times that night feeling his hands around my throat"]*

    *I awoke the next day in a fog but I had to get to work
because I was under a subpoena to testify at a hearing. He*

came down to the kitchen and told me he knew he would probably regret it, but he had decided to let me live. However if I ever did anything else to displease him, he would never say a thing, just kill me as I slept. My digestive problems started that day.

That week passed in a fog. When the following Monday came, he told me we were not returning to counseling. I called the counselor on Tuesday to tell her and she asked what had happened. After I told her, she told me it was dangerous for the kids and me to stay there because he was decompensating and she had seen it coming for a long time. She referred me to Rena Bishop at the Council for Battered Women.

It took 24 hours for me to get the courage to call Rena. I was in a state of shock, realizing the ramifications of what I had heard. When I called at first she was unavailable and another counselor asked if she could help. When I told her why I was calling, she started asking about my financial situation and referred me to the Salvation Army's shelter, since I could afford to pay. After that I would only talk to Rena. I was immediately impressed by her compassion and directness. I had no opportunity to be wishy washy about what I wanted to do. She referred me to attorney John Sweet, mentioned his reputation for handling divorces where protection was an issue. I was instructed to try to see him on Thursday then to get back with her.

I couldn't see John until 2:00 Friday. His personality was an extension of Rena's. By 4:00 he had dictated my divorce and the protective order. He wanted me out of the house that evening, but I didn't have time. He decided I should be in his office at 9:00AM Monday, but that was a holiday and my husband was home, so we settled on 9:00AM Tuesday. His final question to me was "do you think you can hold him off over the weekend?"

I did. It was the hardest thing I've ever done. I would sit and try to plan what I would do, and he would look at me and ask what I was thinking. He talked about how skinny I was and that I needed to "fatten up" and we visited his mother.

The day of my escape was dreary, rainy, and cold. I had gone into my daughter's room the evening before and told her we were leaving and to stack together things she wanted to take, and that I would pick her up from school. My son woke up sick. I helped him dress and left him in bed. My husband left about 7:30. I had an hour before I had to leave for John's office. It took me an hour and 20 minutes. I took winter coats etc. to a friend's house, hurriedly threw things in my car, and got my son and the dog.

I was scared. We went from John's office to the courthouse. Everything was filed. I knew that I had to call Rena. My son thought we were on a holiday, so I decided to spend the first night in a hotel. I was afraid to be on the streets.

(My husband frequently came home in the middle of the day.) When we settled in at the hotel I started trying to reach Rena. She told me I should try to find a friend for my daughter (since she was older than most kids there) and that my son and I should come immediately. I told her that I would come the following day, but she indicated that she could not guarantee that a room would be available. When I picked my daughter up she had good news. A classmate had asked her to stay at her house. The next day the shelter was full. Rena referred us to a church operated one. (It happened to be near my husband's place of employment.) By then my fear of being on the streets had tripled. We were there only two hours when Rena called to say a room at the Council's shelter was available for us.

I was pleasantly surprised to see that the shelter wasn't institutionalized and it reminded me of a college dorm— but with kids. We had the "best" room. Even so, it was quite an adjustment after leaving a 4 bedroom house. Intake was my first order of business. The reaction to my educational level, position and salary was interesting. I heard choruses of "you make more than I do," and "I don't have my MSW yet," and "maybe you can help me get a job." Intake ended with them concluding that there was nothing I needed them to do for me because I didn't need legal aid, welfare, public housing, or a job. I was too tired mentally and physically to argue. What I really needed then was a cup of tea. . . .

I was given a list of "rules" which I read and left on my own. Supper was being prepared and for the first time in weeks I felt hungry. I heard someone yelling it was ready and I ventured into the dining area. I stood around and watched for a few minutes then decided I should pick up a plate and sit down. I couldn't eat much.

THAT'S AS FAR AS SHE GOT. IN THE MIDST OF WRIT-ing, she must have still had hope—if not absolute faith—that her story was a story of escape, of starting anew, that there was a happy ending still ahead of her, that she was indeed living it. I think of Orson Welles's words: "If you want a happy ending, that depends, of course, on where you stop your story."

11.

HALLELUJAH

MY MOTHER IS FLYING. SHE IS SMILING, HER SLEN-der arms undulating as if they are wings, as if she is a bird. It is high summer, 1984. Morris Day and the Time play on the radio. The song—her new favorite—is "The Bird." She dances as if she's free to soar like one. And finally (*Squawk, Hallelujah!*), she is. I have not seen her this untethered in years. She does not say it, but we are celebrating. Joel is in prison, nearly a yearlong sentence ahead of him, and she is, for the first time in ten years, free.

In this moment we are far from the night in the fall of 1983 when my mother put into action her plan to escape. "Put everything you want to take with you in the front of your closet and stacked on your dresser," she'd said. "Don't take the bus home from school. I'll pick you up." I needed no explanation. Perhaps I had seen it coming: not in her stoic face, the usual smile she offered me, but something unusual in her behavior during the preceding weeks.

She and I had spent very little time together during my years in high school, and so I did not know what to make of her sudden show of attachment to me, one evening, when I went to the kitchen to announce that I needed to walk up the street on an errand. Joel was sitting at the table, his long legs crossed, watching her wipe down the counter—his face angled so that he could regard her with his left eye, which seemed to bulge even more when he was angry. They seemed not to have been talking as I came down the stairs, or perhaps just speaking too quietly for me to hear them. It was a small gesture that struck me, something girlish in the way she cried, "I'll go with you!" And how tightly she held my hand as we walked, swinging it a bit, as I'd done long ago, a small child skipping beside her.

The feel of her hand in mine might as well have been a conduit. Before I knew it I was telling her, at last, all the things I had been holding back for years. *He torments me when you are not at home*, I heard myself saying. *I used to be able to stay in my room on Saturday mornings when you went shopping, pretending I was asleep until you returned. But now he just comes into my room and starts harassing me as soon as you leave the house.*

It was not long after that, on a Monday evening in October, that she knocked on my door and came quietly into the room, her arms crossed as if she were holding herself as she spoke. I was lying on my bed, reading. When I think of this now, I hear only my own voice in my head—*Put everything you want to take with you in the front of your closet and stacked on your dresser. Don't ride the bus home from school. I'll pick you up.* I have only a visual image of her, the sound of her voice long gone each time the scene replays: I watch her move stiffly, thinner in her yellow bathrobe than she's ever been, as she turns and walks back down the hall toward the room where I know he is watching TV, waiting for her.

I will go to sleep, I remember thinking, *and when I wake I will never see him again*. But then I did. Less than a week later, unable to find her, he came to the place he knew I'd be on a Friday night: the high school football game at Panthersville Stadium. I was down on the track that runs around the field with the other cheerleaders when he walked onto the landing from the doorway to the concessions stand. There were only a handful of people who knew what was going on—among them, my best friend and her father, who sat directly in front of me, a few rows up, watching to see if Joel would come. I can't remember why we assumed that he would—perhaps it made sense that he would try to get a message to my mother in the women's shelter he'd not yet been able to find.

I spotted him at the top of the stadium, in the doorway, and watched him—though I pretended not to—as he made his way down the bleachers. He had that wild look I'd seen before, his Afro misshapen and his left eye bulging from its socket, larger than the other. When he chose a seat just in front of my friend and her father, I could no longer pretend not to notice him, so I waved, smiling and mouthing the words, "Hey, Big Joe."

HEY, BIG JOE, I'D SAID TO HIM. AFTER THAT, HE didn't stay much longer.

Years later I would read in the court documents that he told his psychologist at the VA hospital he'd brought a gun with him, planning to kill me right then and there, on the track around the football field, to punish my mother. He hadn't, he said during his trial, because I'd waved and spoken kindly to him.

I did not yet know how that scene would haunt me over the years—before I'd ever read his words—my gesture toward him some kind of betrayal of my mother.

Had I known it even then, known it in my body first, that something I'd done had changed the course of events? Had he killed me then, as he claimed to have intended, he would have been apprehended, convicted, and imprisoned. By smiling and speaking a greeting to him, I had unwittingly saved myself.

BY DECEMBER, AFTER HER PETITION TO THE COURT, the divorce she requested was final and my mother, Joey, and I had moved into our new apartment on Memorial Drive in Stone Mountain. She'd waited until the decree was signed before we went back to the house to gather the rest of our things and clean it out to put on the market to sell. We had to work quickly because Joel had checked himself into the VA hospital, from which— against the recommendation of the psychiatrist—he could sign himself out at any time. She put me in charge of clearing out the basement, where there were boxes of old files that needed to be sorted. Though I never told her, this was when I discovered that Joey is in fact my half brother, not just my stepbrother as I had thought. I stared for a long time at the birth certificate that listed her as "mother," unable to fathom why she'd never told her own mother. Like me, my grandmother believed that Joey was another woman's biological son.

The shock of learning that secret was soon replaced by the embarrassment I felt when I went outside to put some things in the moving van. My mother had taken every one of Joel's pornographic magazines from behind the bar in the den and piled them on the curb beside the mailbox. There must have been five stacks, each one four feet tall. Watching the neighborhood boys grabbing as many as they could hold before riding away on their bikes, I was overcome with shame.

My mother seemed unfazed as she went about putting more things we were discarding at the curb. It was as if, once she'd decided to flee, she no longer cared about keeping the foul secrets of that house. She was making a full disclosure: the truth of our lives with Joel now out in the open, in broad daylight, right beneath the nameplate on the mailbox. GRIMMETTE.

I SETTLED EASILY INTO MY NEW LIFE. IT WAS MY senior year of high school, and I could now drive myself back and forth to the campus for classes and cheerleading or gymnastics practice. In the afternoons I'd come home without having to worry that Joel might be there. Instead of heading straight to my room, I could now sit in the kitchen or on the screened-in porch, reading and drinking tea. My favorite afternoon snack was a hunk of crusty bread and some lovely cheese that my mother would leave for me. Placed in delicate symmetry on a bright white plate and drizzled with a bit of honey, the food seemed a beautiful manifestation of the quiet order she'd made for me after so many years of chaos. On the refrigerator she would have posted the weekly breakfast and dinner menu. For the first time in years everything felt normal—though to any of my teachers observing my behavior at school, nothing would have seemed any different. Like my mother with her coworkers, I had never told any of them what went on in that house we'd fled.

Things were harder for my brother, and my mother had been taking him to see a child psychologist to deal with the trauma of separation. He had trouble in school and was frequently sullen. One day, to make Joey happy, she agreed to buy him a pair of shoes he'd been asking for—even though they did not come in children's sizes. I remember being in the car as she drove around the city for hours, trying to find a pair of blue suede Adidas sneakers in a size small enough for his feet. It was

a few weeks before Christmas, and when Donny Hathaway's "This Christmas" came on the radio, she turned it
up and sang along so happily that I began to imagine it
would be the anthem for all our Christmases to come.
Now, much as I love the song, I can't hear it without
weeping—joy tinged with grief.

WE ONLY HAD TWO SHORT MONTHS OF RESPITE BE-
fore Joel made his first attempt to kill her, on Valentine's
Day 1984. That morning, I was in my room at the back
of the apartment getting dressed for school when Joey
knocked on the door. He'd been sitting at the kitchen
table, eating his breakfast. "I just saw Mama and Daddy
get in the car and drive away together," he told me. I
knew immediately something must be wrong, and I
think he must have sensed it too, but I didn't want to let
on that I was worried. "OK," I said. "Go back and finish
your breakfast. I'll take care of it."

I called my grandmother first, then the battered wom-
en's shelter. The woman on the phone listened quietly as
I described what my brother had seen. "Maybe they just
went somewhere to talk," she said.

I was not happy with that response. I knew that the
people at the shelter should know better and, this time,

I wanted someone to respond in the right way to what I was saying, to *do* something.

"No," I said. "My mother would never get in the car and go anywhere with him. Never."

After the calls, I got Joey to the bus stop and then left for school. It's odd to me that I don't recall anything about being at school the few hours before I finally heard from my mother. I recall only the moment I saw her again that evening. She seemed tired and moved slowly, limping a bit. She winced when I hugged her.

The detail that has always stayed with me—from what little she told me of her ordeal that day—is that there was a knock on the door of the apartment, to which Joel had brought her once he could assume Joey and I had left for school. She told him she needed to answer the door because she had asked maintenance to repair the dishwasher. Before that, she had been stalling him, trying to prolong her life, even buying some time by having sex with him when he blamed her for his impotence. And then the knock came. Nothing had been wrong with our dishwasher and she had not called for repairs, but she knew Joel would expect the repairman to let himself in if no one answered. No, that knock could only have been the police and, in that moment, she said, she knew that she'd been saved.

DeKalb County Police Department

CASE NO. 84-037377

STATEMENT OF: Gwendolyn Grimmette

ADDRESS: 5400 Memorial Dr. Apt. 18D

SEX: F

HGT: 5'7³/₄"

WGT: 117

RACE: B

Statement taken by Inv. H.P. Brown

DATE 2-14-84

TIME 11:03

On February 14, 1984 at approximately 7:15AM
I left my apartment and was about to get in the
State car. Joel Grimmette Jr., my ex-husband,
came from out of the bushes near my building
and approached me near the state car. I asked
him what he wanted. He said to talk and told me
to get in the car. I refused. He hit me once about
the head. I screamed. He hit me again and said
he had a gun (what appeared to be a gun in the
pocket of his jacket was pointed at me) and if I
screamed one more time he would shoot me then.
I tried to dissuade him by saying our son was
watching out of the window and he turned and
waved at him. Then he took the keys to the car,
opened the passenger side, and forced me in. By

*then I saw that he had a knife. I told him it was
illegal for him to drive a state car, but he wouldn't
listen. I asked where we were going; he said he
wanted to talk to me and he would drive me to
work. I asked how he had gotten there, but he
wouldn't answer.*

*He drove down Memorial. As we neared 285,
I told him it would be quicker (to take me to
work) to go straight down Memorial. He took 285
South to Covington Highway, exited, then turned
around to get back on 285 North, and exited
at Memorial. We drove down Memorial to the
Cinema 5 theatre. He turned in there and drove
back to my apartment. He told me to go in, call
my office, and tell them I would be in, but in a
1/2 hour. He listened with his hand on the cord to
disconnect if I said anything else. Then he told me
to sit down—I did on the couch—and to remove
my coat. During all of this time (it was now 7:50,
he had to make sure my kids had gone to school
before we came back) he was talking about hurting
someone close to me: he named my daughter (not
his daughter) and my mother. He said he had been
following her, my daughter, (he had previously told
me he was following me, too) and could shoot her
anytime. He told me to go to the bedroom, and*

sit on the bed. I did. He struck me in the mouth,
near the eye, and about the head several times with
his fist. I began screaming. He hit me again in the
kidney, said he would break my back if I didn't
shut up.

I was trying to reason with him, and he
continued to say I couldn't be trusted and that he
should have killed me before I left him, etc. etc.
Then he asked if I knew how I was going to die.
I said no. He said it would be real peaceful, and
took out a needle with clear liquid in it. He asked
if I knew what it was. I said no. He began talking
about me taking everything from him, and that
he was now impotent. I took that as a cue and
followed up, by suggesting that it wasn't true, in
order to buy some time. I told him he should not
die (by then it was going to be a murder suicide).
He told me he had a key to my apartment and had
been in. He proved it by reciting some personal
mail he had read of mine. He lit a cigarette then,
a skinny one. I asked if it were pot; he said yes. I
asked when he had started smoking it; he indicated
since I left. He pulled some string (bits of cloth)
from his pocket and tried to tie my hands. We
struggled, he hit me, threw me across the bed on
the floor and kicked me.

At that point I became extra fearful. Because
he admitted that the psychiatrist said he should
stay in the hospital. He even said he had gone in
Friday of last week, so he wouldn't be around to
"watch me." I convinced him to have sex before
he died. He did. Then I told him I wouldn't want
Joey to come home to that scene and he should take
me somewhere else. He said I would run, but not
to worry, he would "remove" my body. Then he
took the needle and started pushing it in my arm.
I was trying to convince him to get help, telling
him over and over that I would work with him.
He refused, said he wanted the "easy" way out, that
he would be dead by tomorrow and maybe we'd
meet one day in the great beyond. By that time the
policeman knocked on the door. I told him it was
maintenance—that they would come in anyway—
and grabbed my robe, and ran to the door with
him telling me to wait, and opened it.

GWENDOLYN GRIMMETTE

After Joel's conviction, the feeling of relief I'd had
when we first escaped came back. This time he was no
longer in our world. There would be no chance of encountering him on the street, no way that he could get
to us.

For the first time in so many years, all the years they were married, my mother and I were growing close again—just as we had been when I was a small child our first few months in Atlanta. This is why, in the scene that comes back to me again and again, she is dancing and I am laughing and clapping along to the song. It is high summer, 1984, Morris Day and the Time on the radio, doing "The Bird."

And, finally, my mother is soaring, her winged joy boundless and unfettered.

12.

DISCLOSURE

IF YOU HAD TOLD ME EARLY ON HOW MUCH OF MY life I would lose to forgetting—most of those years when my mother was still alive—maybe I'd have begun then trying to save as much as I could. The writer in me now says I'd have been ruthless, keeping a record that could stand as an accurate account of our lives in the years leading up to the tragedy, something that could bring her back to me now, fuller than my memory with all its erasures and revisions. Back then I had already begun to jettison so much, out of a kind of necessity, not knowing there'd be parts I'd want desperately to have again.

Five years after my mother was gone, when I was twenty-four, I found a cassette recording of her voice. It had been long enough that the first things I would come to lose of her had already begun to dissipate—what she smelled like, how she walked—and I felt that I was enacting a kind of betrayal, letting her go in pieces. The tape offered me another chance to resurrect and keep some part of her this time—willing myself to do so, rehearsing the memory of her voice. Perhaps I could learn to imitate it and, like a ventriloquist, project her words out of my own mouth.

Even though I found the tape in my grandmother's house—far back in the old record console, with its stacks of blues 78s and a turntable that had long since ceased to work—I didn't tell her about it. I wanted my mother all to myself, so I took the cassette player into the front bedroom, the one I'd shared with my parents when I was small, the same one I had stayed in each summer before and after my mother was dead, and pressed Play.

I could see her then in the glow of hurricane lamps on the dresser, applying lipstick, her back to me, her face reflected in the mirror. I could see the cameo she wore, nestled like a jewel in the hollow of her throat, the black velvet choker that held it in place, its little gold chain dangling at the back of her neck making her look like a doll—one whose voice could be heard only by pulling that chain and releasing it.

Her voice. After I'd pressed Play my mother came back to me for less than thirty seconds before the tape snagged in the machine, her voice garbled, and stopped. I took the cassette out and wound the tape gently, flattening the length of it as I went. But each time I put it back in to play it would catch before I could hear her utter another word. I kept taking it out, smoothing it over and over, stretching it between my fingers until the worn tape snapped in my hands. Had I waited, I might have been able to save it. The length of tape that held her voice had been as tenuous as the faith that held Orpheus and Eurydice together as he tried to lead her out of the underworld.

In my impatience, I had severed it.

13.

EVIDENCE

Tape of Recorded Conversations, June 3 and 4, 1985

IN THE DAYS LEADING UP TO HER DEATH, MY mother worked with the DeKalb County District Attorney's office of the Stone Mountain Judicial Circuit to gather evidence that would compel a judge to issue a warrant for Joel's arrest. Since his release from prison, he had been calling her repeatedly and, as the record states, "making terroristic threats." What the DA needed was evidence of those threats—not simply her word—so the assistant DA installed a recording device in her apartment, connected to her phone. Each time Joel called, she would have to operate it manually, disabling it when she took other personal phone calls.

In the condensed transcript that follows, there is an interruption to one of her conversations with Joel: my call from school to let her know when exams would be over and when she could pick me up for summer vacation. It was June 4, 1985, the last time I spoke with her.

The State v. Joel T. Grimmette
Tape of Telephone Conversation of June 3, 1985

GWEN: Hello.

JOEL: Hi.

G: Hi.

J: I really feel good today, I feel like I've got a new meaning, a new purpose in life.

G: Why is that?

J: I guess what you told me this morning.

G: Now, what exactly are you assuming from whatever?

J: Well, you said that you was gonna give me a chance.

G: No, I didn't.

J: I thought—

G: You asked me last, the last thing you—

J: I know, I said, us—"Would you do one thing for me, would you think about it?" You said, "I already did."

G: And I said I would continue to think, that's exactly what I said, Joel.

J: I thought, I mean, you said "I already did," and uh, "I will."

G: Joel, I think you're hearing what you want to hear.

J: Unh-uh.

G: Joel, I've been trying to explain to you again and again that the same problems that have always existed are still there for me, all right? I am still basically terrified of you.

J: I, I, I can't help that [*unintelligible*] because I know you have been recently, but what I've got, I, I can't [*unintelligible*] but I have the same fear.

G: Same fear of what?

J: You.

G: I don't quite understand that. I, I never tried to hurt you. I never threatened you.

J: Yeah, you hurt me—mentally not physically, but mentally.

G: You mean when I left?

J: Right.

G: Joel, what options did I have?

J: Gwen, things was getting better.

G: No, no, no, they were *not* getting better, remember? That's when your threats had accelerated, you remember.

J: No, I have been bending over backwards trying to work things out with you.

G: Don't you recall that one of the last things that happened the last week I was there is that you had said to me that, um, you know, if ever I did

anything that displeased you, you weren't ever going
to say anything, you were just going to wait until I
went to bed and end it during the night. That's what
happened that very last week.

J: That was because you had said, you had got up and
told that lady that you wanted a divorce, and, and
I had been working real hard, I had been doing
everything that you asked me to do. I did everything
that you had asked me to do, and you just, you
know, you just cut me up.

G: Joel, you, you saw what had happened to me
physically, how much weight I had lost—you knew
I was having chronic diarrhea and loss of appetite.
I couldn't stay in a situation like that. I had to get
away. I had asked you at that time for just a, um, a
separation and you wouldn't agree to that. You told
me you'd rather see me dead.

J: You realize what's been happening to me?

G: What do you mean?

J: I'm just a shell right now, I have no insides at all.

G: I'm, you know, after all that has happened, I still
don't hate you. You know I told you that last night.
I guess it's just not in my nature and I, I'm, I'm not
happy to hear that you're suffering. But I, and—
maybe I sound selfish to say—I've got to look after,
out for me, too. I— Do you not understand?

J: I'm looking out for you also.

G: What do you mean?

J: Like I told you this morning, I'm desperate now, I've got to the point where I am afraid for me for anybody around [*unintelligible*]. I misunderstood you this morning, but I thought you had said that you was going to give me another chance. My whole life would just brighten up.

G: I have been really trying to be just as cooperative as I could, you know, and, and, talking to you and letting you and Joey have as much time as you could together—

J: And I appreciate that, and, and, that was good for me, but that wasn't enough. I still felt separated from my family. I know you don't consider yourself as part of my family, but I always consider you as a part of my family.

G: Why?

J: Because I, just from the very beginning, I always told myself if it wasn't for you there wasn't gonna be anybody. And I needed that, I needed you. I still need you.

G: Don't you think that, that, that obsession is a little bit unhealthy?

J: Maybe so, but I can't help it, I'm dying to see you. Dying, I am dying every day a little more . . . I

mean . . . Sometimes I'm laying here in my bed
thinking I, you know, I can't take it no more. I'm
just gonna go ahead and do away with us; I'm
not gonna even try to talk to her because all she's
trying to do is try to bide time and, damn, I'll
be just laying again thinking that things are okay
[*unintelligible*]. And then you change your mind,
and then when I try to talk to you on the phone you
say, "Well, I don't, I have nothing to say to you until
after you get some help." Even then I was thinking,
"Well maybe she really thinks that I need help."

G: Are you saying that you don't think you do, Joel?
Rage and violence and threats and intimidation are
not a normal way of life. You're not in Vietnam.

J: No, I'm not.

G: And, and the thing that I'm afraid of is that, that,
knowing that that rage lives under the surface that
it'll erupt at any time for any reason. Just look,
just look at yesterday and Saturday and all of the
things that you were saying then, and you don't
understand?

J: I understand, yes, I do. I didn't do anything . . .
and to me, the way I was feeling, I had plenty of
opportunities to do something to you. And I kept
telling myself, "I've got to, I've got to let her know.
I've got to have this, I've just got to have a chance to

show her." I feel like this kid who's been practicing
playing ball all his life and the coach sit him on the
bench. And you know you can get out there, you
know you can do it, but you just don't have the
opportunity, all because you messed up one other
time. And I just don't feel it's fair to me.

G: Joel, it wasn't just one time, it was ten years' worth.
Come on . . .

J: Yeah, but, I, what you failed to realize is that out
of all those ten years, maybe yes I did make a lot
of mistakes, but what I'm saying now is I won't
be doing that anymore; the communication is
gonna be better. I mean we're gonna be able to
talk, discuss things, things, you know. You— I'm
not putting anything on you, but you're guilty of
not communicating with me either, and yes, I was
showing temper today, but it's gonna be different
because we're gonna work together.

G: Right, let me explain something to you. There
has to be some basis for working together. First of
all, there has to be a mutual decision on the parts
of both people that they want to build that kind
of relationship together. You have decided that,
and what you're telling me, or what you told me
yesterday is I had better decide or my options had
run out.

J: Oh, well, yeah, yeah, you gave me the same choice,
you told me that if we go to see a marriage counselor
and things would get better. I did that, I worked
with you. And, you let me down. You—

G: What the marriage counselor did for me was
help me see that I just didn't want to stay there. I
didn't know that when I went into the marriage
counseling, but it just—

J: You had made up your mind before we even went in
there.

G: No, I hadn't.

J: That was your way of hoping that they could
convince me.

G: You've always said that, and I guess you'll always
believe it.

J: I felt like I was tricked.

G: Yes, I remember you saying that.

J: It was the hurtin'est thing in my life when you said
that and I, I, I just couldn't—I just couldn't stand it.

G: Joel, you've, you've just really—as the saying goes—
put me between a rock and a hard place.

J: You know, it would seem wrong or bad for you, but
even now, what I'm . . . I'm gonna make it up to you.

G: How are you going to make it up to me, Joel? You've
given me no choice in this. You can't go into a
relationship like that.

J: I've waited eighteen months, you know, and you say I'm impatient.

G: Eighteen months, you had nothing to wait for. It's not like I had said to you, "Oh, come on out of jail, Joel, and we're going to start all over again." You built that fantasy all by yourself.

J: It's gonna work. I know it's gonna work. It's got to work.

G: Why?

J: Because I'm gonna work my ass off to make sure that it does.

G: Joel, I'm not going to get into it. I can't get into it, Joel.

J: Gwen, [*unintelligible*] stop thinking about yourself.

G: Who am I thinking about?

J: Just you, that's all you're thinking about right now. You know you told me, I *asked* you not to leave me, and you thought about it. You said, "Okay, I thought about it and I decided we'll try to work it out." And you didn't, you know. Granted, I did a lot of things that I'm ashamed of, I'm guilty of, but when you're weak and desperate you know, you're not *rational*. And I know it's not right to try to force you into trying to work something out, but at this point, since you can't make up your own mind to see that this is gonna work, I have no choice but to

try to force you and I feel in a short period of time
that you would say, "I see now and I'm glad that you
[*unintelligible*]."

G: Joel, you're living in a fantasy.

J: Maybe I am but it's the only world that I have
right now.

G: Why won't you try to get out of it?

J: The only way I know to get out of it is to take my
life, and I'm not gonna leave this world and leave
you behind. I want, I mean, we're gonna have to go
together. I don't want you to suffer, thinking like I
did before. I want to take you with me if I have to
go. And maybe in the next world we'll still be
together.

G: I have never understood one thing about you: how
you could hurt people that you say you love.

J: I'm not gonna hurt you, I'm just gonna take you
with me—that's not *hurting* you.

G: Joel, what do you mean that's not hurting me?
Shooting me or cutting me or something *will*
hurt me.

J: Gwen, we made a vow "till death do us part."
When we made that vow, I made it with my heart,
and I thought you did, too. There's nothing wrong
with wanting to spend the rest of your life with a
person. . . . Give me a fresh start.

G: But Joel, what you're saying now is that if I don't give you a fresh start then you're going to kill me, I mean that's what you're saying.

J: I, I, well . . . the chances of me losing complete control are greater now than they were back in February. Sure, I can probably control myself, but at this point, I don't *want* to because I don't want to live without you.

G: Why do you think it's greater now than in February? I thought you were under better control now.

J: Because for thirteen months I have told myself every day I woke up, I said I was gonna kill you when I got home. And I would ask myself why, and I would say because if I can't have her, nobody will. If I'm gonna die, I'm gonna take her with me. And I told myself that for thirteen months, every day, not just one time a day but that stayed on my mind. Locked up in that one little room cell I had nothing to do but think. I have embedded these things in my head that only you can take out.

G: And—

J: Sure, it's probably gonna be rough for you the first minute, but things will get better and eventually it will go away.

G: Does it matter to you that, that there's no love there?

J: Then love will come. Your kind of love, it will come. There was no love there for ten years. [*Sigh*]

G: You just really don't give me any choices.

J: I'm giving you two roads to travel. You are at the fork now. Don't make the same mistake I made for ten years.

G: I don't quite understand the forks. The mistake you made for ten years was what? Choosing the wrong fork, is that what you're saying?

J: Yes, and I suffered dearly for it.

G: And?

J: And I'm, you know, I'm offering you more than, you just don't realize what I'm offering.

G: You talking about life?

J: Things would be better for Joey, for you, for me, I'll be motivated, I'll just know I'll be conscious of everything that's going on around. I want you to think about the bad part, how it's always gonna be there.

G: That's what you see on one fork?

J: On the other fork, sadness for everybody.

G: Have you thought about how your hurting me would affect the children?

J: Yes, I have.

G: And that doesn't matter to you?

J: Yes, it matters to me. It means a lot to me about how, but they'll, they'll have to accept it just like

when your mother dies: you won't want to accept it
but you'll have to accept it because you know that
we're not put here on earth to last forever.

G: Joel, you can't correlate those things. You know,
natural death is one thing. That's not what you're
talking about.

J: But I've died one time already for you.

G: I'm not sure I understand what that means.

J: When you divorced me, I died inside.

G: Oh, come on, Joel. We're talking about leaving this
earth. Now stop being whatever you're being. We're
talking about the kids' mother dying a natural death
versus you killing me. Now how can you correlate
those two things?

J: What I'm saying is that eventually they will get over
it. It will probably be with them the rest of their
lives, but I think they will adjust to it. They will have
to. And then, if they don't, you could be as much to
blame as I would be.

G: Why?

J: Because it didn't have to be that way.

G: And you really think that any two people, any two
rational adults, can even start a relationship or try to
start a relationship on this basis?

J: At this point, well, we don't have a choice.

G: "We"?

J: We don't.

G: Why?

J: Sometimes you have to force people to see that they're making a mistake. Sometimes they're so geared to believing things sometimes and, and, and, and, and you have to, to, to not convince them, but you have to put them in the position where they have no choice.

G: Joel, please don't force me into this.

J: Into what?

G: Into making a decision for any other reason than it's because I want to do it.

J: You know, I've waited and waited and things are at a standstill. They stayed that way. You know, I'm at the point now you've heard the expression, shit or get off the pot. I can't endure it any longer, you know. I told you how good I felt when I misunderstood you. Damn it, I wish you could have felt what I felt. Then you would understand. I couldn't understand why the nonacceptance—no for an answer. Because you realized what this is gonna mean. A whole new life, a whole new way of life. A chance to be a family with the people you love.

G: Joel, you're living in a fairy tale.

J: Maybe I am, but it's my fairy tale. And fairy tales do come true if you work hard at it. I believe that anything that you want to happen will happen as long as you have faith in yourself, and a willing mind to do it. That's why, you know, it would be easy for me to make you happy.

G: And just as easy for you to kill me.

J: I have convinced myself it's gotta be one way or the other, no other way. I don't want to die, but I don't want to keep going on the way I am.

G: Joel, I don't want to die, either, but I don't want you to force me into this decision.

J: I, I can't help it. You won't make it on your own. You, you, you don't—you *won't*—so I have to force you, so that [*unintelligible*]. How are you getting to work tomorrow?

G: I don't know yet, I'll have to bum a ride.

J: Do you want me to come pick you up?

G: No.

J: Why?

G: Joel, I told you, I'm afraid to be around you.

J: I know that, but the only way you're gonna overcome that fear is to be around me. Being locked up in that little box there's no solution. You know, it might be peace of mind for you but for a while. But you've got to come out, you've got to reach out. Gwen? Gwen?

G: What?

J: I said, "Okay"?

G: Joel, I, I, I'm just going to hang up.

J: I wish you wouldn't.

G: I'm just going to hang up.

J: I wish you wouldn't. Gwen, we're running out of time. You've procrastinated enough. You're just stalling.

G: Joel, you—

J: I know you. I can read you like a book. And all you've got to do is just say, "Okay, we'll try."

G: Joel, and then when I say I did it because I was scared, you'll get mad and say I lied to you again, and we're back to square one.

J: No, no. No.

G: If I said it at this point, Joel, that's the only reason it would be.

J: Okay, at this point I'll take it any kind of way.

G: Joel, you just can't force people into doing what you want them to do.

J: Quit stalling, Gwen, just give me an answer.

G: That's my answer.

J: So you don't want to live.

G: Joel, of course I want to live.

J: So aren't you gonna do what I want?

G: I'm going to hang up and take something for my stomach, all right?

J: Okay, well, what about tomorrow? Do you want me, can I come take you to work?

G: No, Joel, I'll, I'll get to work okay. Please don't come over here.

J: Yeah, but I need, I haven't seen you in two weeks. When will I get a chance to see you, to sit down and talk to you?

G: My preference would be in the presence of a third party, because I'm, I'm still terrified.

J: No, that's not gonna work.

G: Why?

J: The third party could be Joey. And the first few times you're gonna be afraid, you're gonna be nervous. I'm gonna be nervous. But it's gonna also be exciting.

G: It's not going to be exciting, it's going to be terrifying. And you just, just better well realize that.

J: It's gonna be great. And, and, in the long run, you'll learn to like me and then you'll learn to love me.

G: That's a fairy tale.

J: It's mine.

G: You can call Joey when he gets home tomorrow and tell him what the arrangements are, all right?

J: Okay, I love you Gwen. Hello?

G: Oh, goodbye.

J: I love you.

G: No you don't.

J: Yes I do.

G: You could not say you're going to kill me if you love
me, Joel.

J: I, I, I've known, not personally, a lot of people who
have taken their lives for the person they loved
because they couldn't live without them. It happens
every day somewhere. But we are lucky, we are gonna
be able to work ours out, you'll see. I love you.

G: Goodbye.

J: Bye-bye.

[When the call ends, my mother records the time and date.]

G: This is Gwen Grimmette, it's 8:26 on June 3, 1985.
I just finished with—[*abrupt end*]

The State v. Joel T. Grimmette
Tape of Conversation of June 4, 1985

*[My mother must have had trouble engaging the device,
so the conversation had already started when the recording
begins.]*

JOEL: All right, well what, I mean—what happened?

GWEN: Joel, nothing happened. You know, you know
how many years ago I used to tell you that you make

me do things out of fear, and that's just not right,
Joel. Let me let Joey in, hold on a second.

J: That's not true, okay.

G: It's the same old, same old. You've never given me
any choices, you always—

J: Damn it, I've gave you choices. I gave you a lot
of choices. You chose to hurt me, Gwen. I had no
other, I had no other choice but this way. You, you
let me down again. Last night you said you would
[go to dinner], now you're letting me down again.

G: And I told you last night, Joel, that by saying that it
was only because I felt you had me between a rock
and a hard place and—

J: And now you don't feel like I have you?

G: Of course I do, but I just—

J: You just don't mind dying, do you? You know, Joey
asked me. He said, "Don't, don't bother her. You
mad?" I said, "Yes, I'm mad, I'm upset because,
you . . ." So don't let us end this way.

G: Can you hold on a second? I was on the other line.

J: Who, calling the police?

G: No, hold on a minute. . . . *Hello? Hello?* [*Brief pause*]

J: You had your last chance. I don't care what happens
anymore. I tried my best. All I wanted to do was
take you out to dinner, show you a good time and
bring you home and let, and that was it, and maybe

take you out again some other time. And eventually,
gradually, once you find out that I'm not going to
hurt you then it'll be different.

G: But it's *not* any different, Joel, now is it?

J: It *is* different, I'm making it different. You see,
Gwen, I don't have a choice.

G: What do you mean, you don't have a choice?

J: You just want me to go on and forget about you, and
I can't do that. And I'm not going to do it. I told you
last night what my commitment was to myself and to
you. And I intend to carry it out one way or another.

G: Joel, you don't mean that.

J: You ruined my life.

G: I can't hear you.

J: You ruined my life. You owe it to me to spend your
life with me.

G: How do I owe that to you, Joel?

J: Because you ruined mine.

G: I didn't ruin your life, I gave you the best ten years
of mine.

J: And you took a part of me that can't be replaced.

G: And that is?

J: My heart.

G: [*Sighs*] I don't, I don't know how to respond to that.
I mean, people get married and then at another
point they go their separate ways, this isn't unusual.

J: But ours was different. Our, our— I got a divorce
to marry you: I left a son to marry you. I left a good
job for you. I'm what I am today because of you.
You are the cause of that, and you owe it to me. You
obligated yourself.

G: Joel, people aren't possessions.

J: People has nothing to do with this particular time.
I'm talking about me. What belongs to me will
always belong to me. Unless they're dead. And I'm
the same way. I belong to you until I am dead. You
may not want what you see or what I am, but it's
what you made. You created this monster inside of
me. It's your baby, it's yours.

G: I don't believe that monsters once created can't be—

J: What?

G: I don't believe that monsters once created can't be
changed.

J: I have only one way to change it and I tried to get
you to see it that way. You, you, you have no choice;
this is you, yours, you made it. You just can't turn
your back on it and walk away. You have to adjust
and deal with it. And if my mama can put up with
my daddy, you can put up with me.

G: Your mother told me she had no options.

J: You don't have no options at all except for death.
And you keep hollering that you don't want that . . .

G: I don't know what else to say.

J: There's nothing else to say. You, you've said it all.
You said you'd rather die than come back to me.
Now what else is there to say?

G: I never said I'd rather die, Joel. I never said I'd
rather die.

J: You chose death rather than me.

G: Joel, you just, you gave me no options.

J: You had an option. Hell, I didn't ask you to marry
me tomorrow, I just asked you to get close to me.
All I asked you was to go out to dinner. Hell, you
act like I asked you to go spend the whole weekend
with me.

G: You've got to understand, it's just not that easy for me.

J: What?

G: Easy for me.

J: I know. Going to dinner is a hell of a lot easier than
wondering when somebody's going to come up to
you and blow your fucking brains out. Knowing
this maniac's gonna trip and come by and set the
house on fire while you're trapped in there, or do
something to the car so when you turn the ignition
key the damn gas tank blow up. Gwen, you forgot I
spent two years in Vietnam. I can explode anything.
You forget I could go in there and fix your air
conditioner where it will blow up on you tonight.

Not enough to kill you, enough to scare the hell out
of you. You want to live with that?

G: Joel, your son is in here also.

J: Yeah, sometimes you have to make sacrifices. You
love your son?

G: Yes.

J: And you're willing to take the chance on me doing
something to him?

G: To Joey? You wouldn't do anything to Joey.

J: No intentions, I have no intentions, but to get to you
I might overlook the fact that he's in the house and
do something. Gwen, I could bring that apartment,
the whole building down. You, you don't realize that
I am a mechanic working with wires and gas tanks
and, and, and high-pressure valves. Right in your
apartment building is a hot water tank. All I've got
to do is do certain things and that whole building
would go up. You remember Bowen Homes? Huh?

G: Yes.

J: Do you want that to happen?

G: No.

J: And they can't even trace it back to me.

G: You did Bowen Homes?

J: Oh, hell no, I'm talking about after I do *your*
apartment. I'm, I'm, I'm talking about they wouldn't
be able to trace it back, your home. They would

have all the suspicion they want, but you've got to have evidence. You've got to have facts. You saw that didn't you, when we went to court.

G: Huh, yeah, it was just my word against yours.

J: Yeah, but this way it won't be anybody's word against anybody's. Just a freak accident. And it's just a coincidence that it's the apartment that my ex-wife is in. And I've already gotten it on paper that you're a maniac. I mean, you'd lie and do anything to get me put away.

G: What do you mean you've got it I'm a maniac on paper?

J: That you tell lies.

[Whereupon a call interrupts]

G: Hold on.

[Whereupon Gwen Grimmette conducts a personal conversation (with me: the last words between us taking less than a minute)]

G: [*Coming back on the line with Joel*] I didn't tell any lies.

J: You got a fucking man to say I stuck the needle in your arm two or three different times.

G: But you *did*.

J: I did not. I did not break the skin.

G: How can you tell the skin on my arm wasn't broken?

J: I know where I laid the needle.

G: Well why do you think I had the scar there?

J: You probably put it there yourself.

G: I'm not a masochist, I wouldn't hurt myself.

J: Say what?

G: I'm not a masochist, I wouldn't hurt myself.

J: You'd do anything to convince these people.

G: No, I wouldn't. All I did was tell them what happened.

J: And—and you know what?

G: What?

J: I feel, I, I, you can ask Joey. I can come there and make a key to the apartment and come there tonight. I've got bolt cutters that I can cut that little night chain. And I can get in there, I can disconnect the telephone, I can do a lot of things, Gwen. You know that don't you?

G: Yes.

J: And right now you don't know where I am, or how far I am away from your house.

G: That's true.

J: And if I see a police go up in there, I know that you called them and I'll know that I have to act quickly.

G: This is an apartment complex and police are in here all the time.

J: You better hope they don't come in there tonight. Because I'm gonna blame you for it if they do.

G: I can't be responsible for all of the people that live out here, Joel.

J: What do you mean?

G: I, I, I can't be responsible. You can't blame me just because a police car drives in here. Policemen *live* in here.

J: Too bad. Just to show you I'm not bullshitting, I'm gonna come out there and I'm gonna shoot a round through the window, okay. All right?

G: I'm not going to say all right to something like that.

J: I don't think you believe I got a gun.

G: Why shouldn't I believe you have a gun?

J: You don't think that I'm capable.

G: Umm-hmm. Now *that* I definitely believe.

J: Gwen, I, I, I just want to make you happy.

G: I understand, Joel.

J: Who's giving you courage now?

G: Nobody particularly. I've just decided that there's just some, some times in your life that you just have to make a stand.

J: Okay. I guess we have nothing else to talk about.

G: No, I guess we don't.

J: Bye.

G: Bye.

J: One last question.

G: What's that?

J: Under no circumstances would you ever come back to me.

G: Joel, no.

J: Huh.

G: I, I, that's not even anything that we can discuss while you're in this mood. Okay.

J: No, I— Yeah, I, I thought maybe we could compromise since you said I was forcing you to make a decision. You know, if I go and check myself into the hospital and stay until I'm cured, would you consider then?

G: I can't make any promises like that, Joel. I, I have no intentions in that direction.

J: I can't hear you.

G: I said I have no intentions in that direction.

J: So in other words you saying regardless of whatever I do, even if I get cured, you still wouldn't consider it?

G: Joel, you've got to understand that things like this happen every day. People go their separate ways.

J: I know. And I, I believe what caused us to go our separate ways was the fact that I was sick, mentally. And, mental illness can be cured.

G: Are you saying you're going to do that?

J: Yep, if, if, if I felt that there was . . .

G: What?

J: If you told me yes; if you did that, then, yes— I would reconsider.

G: But you're saying you'd rather be running around sick rather than get cured just for yourself?

J: I, I would also ask that, uh, you not involve with anybody while—

G: Oh, come on Joel. You're again trying to dictate my life. You can't—

J: No, I'm not.

G: Yes, you are.

J: All I wanted, I don't want to do anything. All I want is a reason for it. From you.

G: Oh, are you saying you don't want to hurt anybody?

J: No, I don't want to hurt anybody.

G: But I have to give you a reason not to hurt anybody?

J: You gave me a reason to hurt somebody. And my thinking is like this: I've got to, I've got to get some kind of help and you've got to help me.

G: Joel, you've got to get some kind of help, but it's got to be something you want for Joel. It cannot be tied to me. So, please do that.

J: There you go, giving me no hope.

G: I don't want to give you false hope. I want you to decide if you want to be a better person for yourself.

J: Gwen, why did you tell me back in February that,
uh, we would work on it? After you wasn't in no
danger.

G: I wanted to get out of this house in the clear open
air and breathe. I just wanted to get out. . . .

With the evidence obtained in the recorded conversation,
the magistrate issued an arrest warrant at 1:00 a.m. on
June 5, 1985. Still, the police officer posted to watch my
mother's apartment left in the early-morning hours—even
though it was his assignment to stay. Later that morning,
with the police watch discontinued, Joel arrived at her
apartment.

The autopsy records her death from two gunshots, at
close range, in the face and neck. One bullet went through
her raised right hand before entering her head. It lodged
near the base of her skull, behind the bloodred bloom of
her birthmark.

14.

WHAT THE RECORD SHOWS

Hey Joe, where you going with that gun in your hand?
—Jimi Hendrix

THE RECORD SHOWS *MURDER*, SHOWS MAY 31, GETS the day wrong, makes the date she died invisible in the document, takes five days from her, from me, as if they were irrelevant, as if it didn't matter, as if it were not important to be precise, to get it right: She is dead, the imprecision suggests, so what's the difference? She was going to die anyway. May 31, the day he stole the gun, is not the "Hey Joe" day—not the day he said to a co-worker, quoted in the record, "I'm about to kill somebody." Not the day he did.

15.

JUNE 5, 1985

THE VOICE ON THE PHONE SAYS: "MA'AM?" SAYS:
"It's your mother, ma'am. She's been shot."

The police officer standing behind me has told me
almost nothing, only that I must make this call and "get
home as soon as possible." For a moment I do not respond.
I am thinking *shot*, not *killed*, only shot—repeating the
word like a talisman.

Now into the phone I say: "Where is she?" meaning:
Which hospital? "I just need to go to her, 'get home as soon
as possible.'" The room is streaked with morning light
through the blinds, a pattern like a grate on the floor. I
look at it for a long moment, trying to wait out the silence on the other end of the line—a space in which my
mother's living presence grows larger inside me. "Where
is she?" I say again.

And then: "She's dead, ma'am," as if dead were a place.

THE OFFICER WAITS OUTSIDE MY DORM ROOM
while I get dressed. I don't know how long I'll be gone
or what will be expected of me, so I walk around the
room as in a trance, touching things on my shelves, moving books around on my desk, as if the objects, in their
proper places, could realign the world. Then I think of
my grandmother and choose a black dress, pumps, and,
even though it's June and already hot in Georgia, a pair
of black stockings so sheer they cast only a shadow over
my skin. I am of two minds, not wanting to believe what
I have been told, not able to, and yet knowing my grandmother would not want me to go bare legged, irreverent,
into death's formal rooms.

I sit in the back of the police car looking out the
window, trying not to catch the eye of the officer in the
rearview mirror. The route we take, GA 78, is a four-lane
highway, though still a country road near Athens, flanked
mostly by trees, pastures, and—here and there—a clearing with a small roadside stand or market. The officer
tells me he needs to stop for "updates," and when we
come upon a store with a phone booth outside he pulls
over to make a call. I've been counting the miles and
waiting for this, expecting that he will return to the car
to tell me there's been some mistake, that my mother

isn't actually dead—only *shot*—or perhaps that they have identified the wrong woman altogether.

Updates, he'd said. To my mind that can only mean that the situation is changeable, that some other information could come to us that would clear up this terrible mistake. The rest of the trip I am hopeful each time he stops the car to make a call. Hope feels like a balloon inflating inside my chest, expanding the space there until it hurts. Each time he returns to the car and says nothing, I am too afraid to ask him what he has learned. I think it will be better somehow if I, too, say nothing.

The trip takes a little over an hour, during which we make three stops. I spend the time between stops thinking of the last time I spoke to my mother. I'd called her just the previous night, to let her know when my final exams would be over, when she could come to pick me up for summer vacation. She'd sounded rushed on the phone and we talked for less than a minute. I heard what sounded like a series of clicks, the buttons of a machine, a note of distraction in her voice as she spoke to someone else in the apartment.

At the station the officer escorts me inside to a small conference room, telling me I can wait there until my grandmother arrives from Mississippi. There is a small glass panel in the door he shuts behind me, and the back wall is covered in cheap inspirational prints, so I sit there looking at them. I do this to avoid looking at the table before me on which someone has placed my mother's briefcase: a hard shell of oxblood leather, her initials in gold lettering on the top, GTG. I can't help thinking how it seems now an acronym for a phrase I've heard many times in church, especially on Mothers' Day, when daughters pin carnations to their chests: red for mothers still living, white for the dead—Gone to Glory. I'd rather think of this than what I keep pushing away: how only a week earlier I broke my own taboo and uttered these words out loud: *He could come for her and kill her at any time.*

Left alone in the room for several hours, I do nothing but wait, the balloon inside my chest growing heavy as a stone. I can hear the ticking of the wall clock and I force myself to hold out as long as possible before looking up at it again. I resist turning to look through the glass panel behind me. I do not open my mother's briefcase to see what is inside. When my grandmother comes, I can no longer maintain my stoic facade and I lean into her, weeping as she pats my face with a handkerchief. Then I stand next to her, listening to what a police officer is saying: *Joel has not been apprehended. He might be a threat to others.*

They find him in the middle of the night at a motel in a small town south of Atlanta, a place called Griffin.

The clerk had recognized his face from a bulletin on the television news and called the police after giving him keys to a room. When they arrived, Joel still had the gun he'd used to kill her. It lay on the nightstand beside the bed, and as the officers entered the room to arrest him he said he'd planned to use it on himself. Said it as if that fact should elicit their sympathy, that it would somehow lessen the gravity of what he'd done to her.

THE NEXT DAY WE MAKE PLANS TO DRIVE WITH MY father down to Mississippi, where the three of us will meet my mother's body. But first we must go to her apartment to collect some of her things. The only one who knows the way around Atlanta, I give directions from the back seat, looking out at the city passing before me as if it were a place I'd never seen.

Entering the parking lot of the apartment complex, I see what's left of the chalk outline on the pavement where her body had lain. There is a stain that travels downhill from the spot, a dark rivulet alongside the white curb. In front of the apartment a television news crew waits beside a van. As we walk by, the reporter asks to interview us, but my grandmother shakes her head without speaking and my father waves the crew away. There is yellow police tape still stuck to the apartment door when I pass through it.

Inside we walk around, searching, though no one says it, for signs of her last morning: a teacup and saucer in the sink, a few tea leaves—narrative of some inscrutable future—still in the bottom of the cup. But for that, the rooms are unchanged, neat and tidy as always. We do not yet know that the police have removed some items that had been on the kitchen counter: a folding knife, a fifty-cent roll of coins.

Not long after we arrive, the apartment manager knocks on the door asking to send a workman in to clean the carpet. "You know, in case there's any blood," she says. "We can get it out if we act quickly." I barely say anything, but show her the tiny bullet hole in the wall beside my mother's bed, the clean white space around it.

In my mother's closet I search for the outfit in which she'll be buried. Her shoes, a half size smaller and narrower than my own, are arrayed in neat rows, each one hugging a wooden shoe form, little torsos holding the shape of her feet. I choose the black cashmere dress she wore in her last photograph—a formal portrait done in a studio only a few months earlier, framed now and sitting on her dresser. I stand looking at the photograph a long time. I am still staring at it, at the glass in which I see my own reflection within hers, when my father comes into the room to hurry me along. "That doesn't look anything like the woman I knew," he says over my shoulder. "Her mouth is different. I guess he must have punched out her teeth."

LATER, AT A HOTEL DOWNTOWN WHERE WE SPEND the night, the local evening news comes on and I see my likeness on the TV screen. The clip is on a loop as the newscaster speaks, showing over and over the same scene: a young woman walking up to the door of an apartment and stepping in, shutting it behind her.

This is where it begins, our estrangement. For several minutes I watch her, the girl I have left behind, stepping again and again into the last place I saw my mother alive.

16.

JETTISON

CAST OFF, DISCARD, DITCH, DUMP, JUNK, SCRAP, *shed, shuck, slough, toss, deep-six, eighty-six, exorcise.* The objects in her apartment were cargo I could not bear to carry—even the record collection she had loved. That I loved too.

To have it now, I think, might bring some part of her back, hundreds of albums that would play like the soundtrack to the story of her life, the years she lived, taking me back to the moment she first started collecting them, when Uncle Son still had his nightclub and would give her the records he'd bought for the jukebox. Then all the ones she continued to amass over the years—her Temptations and Al Green and Donny Hathaway; her Jimi Hendrix, Marvin Gaye, and Tammi Terrell. Something as simple as her taste in music holding the possibility of revelation.

Back then I wanted nothing of it. Now that I want all of it, one image comes back replacing all the rest: the only album cover I could not bear to look at as a girl, each time I flipped through the stack to find something to play. I would place it randomly among the others, like hiding a card in a deck for a magic trick. Somehow, over and over I'd draw the same one: Funkadelic's *Maggot Brain*.

So this is what stays with me: a woman with an Afro, like the one my mother wore in the early 1970s, buried up to her neck in the dirt, head flung back, her mouth wide open in what looks to be a scream of agony. On the other side of the cover, nothing but a clean white skull. It haunts me now as if to show me the truth of my mother's life those years, foreshadowing what was to come. Her thoughts—everything I couldn't know—locked in her head until she began to unleash them in the last words she wrote, and in that final scream, before her death would render her as bone white, as beyond help, as the woman's head on the album's flip side.

WHAT I WANTED TO GET RID OF WAS THAT IMAGE of captivity and suffering, that final scream.

17.

PROXIMITY

The way you got sideswiped was by going back.

—Joan Didion

ONE EVENING, IN THE SPRING OF 2005, MY HUS-band, Brett, and I are walking into town for dinner at a restaurant on the square in Decatur. Since 2001 we have lived in Decatur, just blocks from the DeKalb County Courthouse, and but for that proximity, I have managed to avoid much of my former life here. I have even begun to relax into the idea that I can continue to do so.

Regulars in the restaurant, we grab a high table in the bar and chat a few minutes with the bartender. We've just gotten our drinks when a man I've never seen approaches us, asks, "Did I just see y'all walking from the hotel?" Because we were coming from home, it doesn't

occur to me that he means *by* the hotel or *near* the hotel that we pass by on our route from home to the restaurant. When I say no he simply apologizes and leaves
us, but within minutes the bartender brings us another
round of drinks and tells us that Bob sent them over,
with his apologies for bothering us.

Brett and I both find this odd, so I decide to go over
to thank him and introduce myself. He is a kind-looking
man with eyes that droop at the outer corners, as if there
is perpetually a deep sadness in him, even when he is
smiling. When I tell him my name he introduces me
to his wife and asks me what I do for a living. We are
engaged in the usual pleasantries and still I have no idea
why he approached us. He tells me he is an assistant district attorney in Rockdale County. "Oh," I say. "Perhaps
you know someone I know, J. Tom Morgan. He used to
be the ADA in DeKalb County."

"How do you know J. Tom?" he asks.

"Well, there was this case years ago . . ." I let my
words trail off and look away from him, out the window toward the courthouse on the square. He pauses for
a long moment before speaking, as if something is just
now dawning on him or that he is readying himself to
say something difficult.

"Was your mother Gwen Grimmette, and Joey your
brother?"

I am stunned by his questions, that he knows who my mother and brother are. I look first to his wife, to see if she seems as perplexed as I am. When I look back at him there are tears welling in his eyes, and then he drops his head and weeps.

"He was the first police officer on the scene," his wife says then. "Not a day passes that he doesn't think about your mother."

This is the year of the twentieth anniversary of her death, the year I have lived more years without her than I did with her. It is the year, Bob tells me, that the courthouse will purge the records of her case, and so he offers to save everything to give to me.

When I meet him a week later, downtown in a bar across from the courthouse, he hands me a big file in a shopping bag and a bottle of wine. "You're going to need it," he says.

I THINK OFTEN OF RALPH ELLISON'S REVISION OF Heraclitus's axiom about the role of character in one's destiny to one about the role of place: "Geography is fate." I had willingly come back to this place, put myself in the proximity of the events of my past. I'd even bought a house in walking distance of the courthouse,

not far from the police station, and but a few miles from
the place my mother was murdered in the shadow of
Stone Mountain, the symbol of the Confederacy and a
monument to white supremacy that joins in my psyche
the geography and history—both public and private, national and personal—of my deepest wounds.

How could I think my past would not revisit me in
countless ways? That I could go unrecognized in this
place? "I saw you that day at the station," Bob told me.
"You looked as though you were already gone, far above
and away from all of it." I know that I must have been
in shock when he saw me, but he clearly detected something else in my face. And now I could see it, too. All
those years I thought that I had been running away from
my past I had, in fact, been working my way steadily
back to it.

[   ]

When I finally sit down to write the part of our story I've most needed to avoid, when I force myself at last to read the evidence, all of it—the transcripts, witness accounts, the autopsy and official reports, the ADA's statement, indications of police indifference—I collapse on the floor, keening as though I had just learned of my mother's death. What comes out is uncontrollable: the long, unbroken primal wailing I never allowed myself back then. So I live it again in real time, only what I am reliving now is not my own feeling of sudden loss, but rather the terror of her last moments.

They could have saved her.

The whole time I have been working to tell this story, I have done so incrementally, parsing it so that I could bear it: neat, compartmentalized segments that have allowed me to carry on these three decades without falling apart.

Three decades is a long time to get to know the contours of loss, to become intimate with one's own bereavement. You get used to it. Most days it is a distant thing, always on the horizon, sailing toward me with its difficult cargo. What I did not expect was to find her last scream, the one several neighbors told the police they heard a moment before two gunshots—her No, No, No— *ringing in my mouth.*

18.

BEFORE KNOWING REMEMBERS

*Some selected image of the past is always being
delivered to our senses.*

—ADRIENNE RICH

OVER THE YEARS, MY MIND HAS TURNED AGAIN
and again to that early memory of my near drowning in
Mexico, the image of my mother above me, arms outstretched, a corona of light around her face. Did I know
then that it reflected an iconic image of the Virgin
Mary? The mind works such that we see and perceive new
things always through the lens of what we have already
seen. What came first, then, the vision of my mother as
I was sinking deeper into the pool, or religious paintings
and altarpieces depicting Mary in much the same way?

What matters is the transformative power of metaphor

and the stories we tell ourselves about the arc and meaning of our lives. Since that day decades ago, the imagery
of the memory has remained the same, I think, because
I have rehearsed it, telling the story of my near drowning again and again. What has changed is how I've
understood what I saw, how I've come to interpret the
metaphors inherent in my way of recalling the events.
Scientists tell us there are different ways that the brain
records and stores memory, that trauma is inscribed differently than other types of events.

To survive trauma, one must be able to tell a story
about it. Thus, if the story I began to tell myself after the
seemingly small trauma of almost drowning was that my
mother had been there, that I was in no real danger, that
she was somehow ethereal, a light-ringed saint to whom I
might send up my prayers for salvation, the story evolved
over the years to create a narrative of self that could in
turn contain yet another trauma and give it meaning.

In *Poetry as Survival*, Gregory Orr asks the survivor's
questions about violence: *How could I have been that
close and not been destroyed by it? Why was I spared?*—
questions that can initiate in a writer the quest for meaning and purpose. "But this quest born out of trauma
doesn't simply lead the survivor forward," he writes.
"First it leads him or her backward, back to the scene of
the trauma where the struggle must take place with the

demon or angel who incarnates the mystery of violence and the mystery of rebirth and transformation." He is referring to Lorca's idea of *duende*: a demon that drives an artist, causing trouble or pain and an acute awareness of death. Of the demon's effect on an artist's work, Lorca wrote: "In trying to heal the wound that never heals lies the strangeness."

So let me go back to that dream I had just after her death, the one that started me on this journey.

Three weeks gone, my mother and I are together again. As if to bring her back, I have journeyed to this place of shadows where we walk, now, side by side, neither of us speaking. Comfortable in our silence, we could go on walking like this forever. But then, out of the darkness, a man emerges, coming toward us. Even in the dream I know that he has killed her, and yet I smile, lifting my hand and speaking a greeting as he passes. "Hey, Big Joe." My mother turns to me then, speaks her last words: "Do you know what it means to have a wound that never heals?" In the center of her forehead is a hole the size of a quarter from which comes a light so bright and piercing it seems I am staring at the sun, her face nothing but light ringed in the darkness that surrounds us. Walking on as before, we meet him again. This time he is holding a gun, aiming at her head. This time I know I must save her, so I throw myself in the bullet's path, shout "No!"—waking now to that single word, my own voice wrenching me from sleep.

IN THAT MOMENT OF WAKING I WAS TRANSFORMED.
The world as I knew it and myself in it were not the
same. Through the metaphor of the dream, I had acknowl-
edged the undeniable presence of my deepest wound.
Had I read Lorca before hearing my mother's last words
in the dream? I doubt that I had. But something of the
past was delivering to me again a familiar scene: that
early image of my mother's face above me, eclipsing the
sun, as I looked up at her from beneath the water's surface. Only now, it was in the negative—a reversal of light
and dark that transformed her face into pure light ringed
in darkness, the light all-consuming and piercing. It was
delivering something else, too: that moment down on
the track around the football field, after we'd run away,
when Joel appeared before me and I smiled, waved, and
spoke a greeting to him: the simple gesture that saved my
life, traded it for my mother's.

Since that first dream, all of my adult life, I have
lived with the guilt that I am implicated in my mother's
death—or, more precisely, that she is dead because I am
not. I did not always know this guilt explicitly, though I
could feel something akin to it gnawing at the edges of
my consciousness.

"Memory knows before knowing remembers," William Faulkner wrote. Over the years, as I applied the dream again and again to the ongoing narrative of my life, I began to see it as a bookend to my earliest memory of trauma—as if my earliest memory had indeed provided the framework of the dream, bracketing the before and after of my life in relation to my mother's death. Being pulled from the water into her arms was akin to a baptism. I had witnessed something strange, not unlike the visions reported by the faithful that set them on a path of devotion, of meaningfulness and purpose: my mother, through the wavering lens of water, seemed distant and not fully embodied—an apparition, the dead woman she was to become, but with the light surrounding her, as if she had already undergone her hagiography.

In the narrative of my life, which is the look backward rather than forward into the unknown and unstoried future, I emerged from the pool as from a baptismal font—changed, reborn—as if I had been shown what would be my calling even then. This is how the past fits into the narrative of our lives, gives meaning and purpose. Even my mother's death is redeemed in the story of my calling, made meaningful rather than merely senseless. It is the story I tell myself to survive.

[   ]

Often, when I am alone on the road, I think of traveling back to Mississippi each summer with my mother. The year before I was old enough to drive, she let me practice steering the car on long stretches of empty highway. I'd reach across the center console and take the wheel, leaning into her, my back against her chest, following the arc of the sun west toward home. For several miles we'd drive like that: so close we seemed conjoined, and I could feel her heart beating against me as if I had not one, but two.

ACKNOWLEDGMENTS

WRITING THIS BOOK HAS BEEN A LONG AND PAIN-
ful journey, and I've had a lot of help from friends along
the way—too many to recount here, so many that I am
bound to forget. I suspect that many of them did not
realize they were helping me in some immeasurable way.
I'll be offering thanks for years to come. This is only
a beginning: Dan Albergotti, Cynthia Blakeley, Jericho
Brown, Rob Casper, Michael Collier, Jean Douglas, Olga
Dugan, Susan Glisson, Alison Granucci, Joe Grimmette
(my brother), Jim Grimsley, Frank Guridy, Daniel Hal-
pern, Leslie Harris, John Hoppenthaler, Kate Johnsen,
Nicole Long, Molly McGee, Pearl and Tom McHaney,
Rob McQuilkin, Don Allen (Chip) Mitchell, ZZ Packer,
Deborah Paredez, Tony and Leisa Powers, Angelo Robin-
son, Michael Taeckens, Charles Tucker, Allen Tullos, Kate
Tuttle, Paula Vitaris, Daren Wang, Lynna Williams, Ce-
cilia Woloch, Jenny Xu, C. Dale Young, Kevin Young,
and—my dearest—Brett Gadsden.